D1794074

```
PS        Etter, Dave, 1928-
3555
.T68       Selected poems
A6
1987


    $14.95
```

		DATE APR 1992	

KVCC KALAMAZOO VALLEY
COMMUNITY COLLEGE
LIBRARY

69196

© THE BAKER & TAYLOR CO.

Dave Etter

Selected Poems

SELECTED POEMS

DAVE ETTER

SPOON RIVER POETRY PRESS
1987

This book is published in part with funds provided by the Illinois Arts Council, a state organization, and the National Endowment for the Arts. Our many thanks.

Selected Poems, copyright (C) 1987 by Dave Etter. All rights reserved. No portion of this book may be reproduced in any manner without written permission of the author, except for quotations embodied in reviews or critical articles.

Published by Spoon River Poetry Press; P. O. Box 1443; Peoria, Illinois 61655.
Typesetting by Rodine the Printer, Peoria, Illinois.
Design and Layout by David R. Pichaske.
Dust jacket photograph by Emily Etter.

ISBN 0-933180-91-8

1 2 3 4 5 6 7 8 9

All characters in this book are fictional, and any resemblance to persons living or dead is purely coincidental.

ACKNOWLEDGMENTS

The poems in this book were previously published in the following collections: *Go Read the River* (University of Nebraska Press), *The Last Train to Prophetstown* (University of Nebraska Press), *Strawberries* (Juniper Press), *Voyages to the Inland Sea* (University of Wisconsin—La Crosse), *Crabtree's Woman* (BkMk Press), *Well You Needn't: The Thelonious Monk Poems* (Raindust Press), *Bright Mississippi* (Juniper Press), *Central Standard Time: New and Selected Poems* (BkMk Press), *Open to the Wind* (Uzzano Press), *Riding the Rock Island Through Kansas* (Wolfsong), *Boondocks* (Crow King Editions), *Home State* (Spoon River Poetry Press), and *Live at the Silver Dollar* (Spoon River Poetry Press).

Most of these poems have also appeared in the following publications: *Abraxas, Ann Arbor Review, Antioch Review, Arbor, The Beloit Poetry Journal, Bluefish, Carolina Quarterly, The Chariton Review, Chelsea, Chicago Daily News, Chicagoland, Chicago Tribune Magazine, Choice, Clockwatch Review, Cream City Review, Cronopios, Dacotah Territory, December, El Corno Emplumado, Elkhorn Review, The Fiddlehead, Focus/Midwest, Genesis West, The Greenfield Review, Hanging Loose, The Husk, Images, The Kansas City Star, Kansas Magazine, Kayak, Long Pond Review, Mad River Review, Maine Times, Mark Twain Journal, Massachusetts Review, Michigan's Voices, Midwest, The Midwest Quarterly, The Minnesota Review, Mississippi Valley Review, New Mexico Quarterly, New Orleans Review, New Work/s, North Dakota Quarterly, Northern Lit Quarterly, Northeast, The North Stone Review, Northwest Review, Ole, Open Places, Parallax, Patterns, Pebble, The Peninsula Review, Poetry, Poetry Northwest, Poetry Now, Prairie Schooner, Puerto del Sol, Quixote, River Bottom, The Salt Creek Reader, Saturday Review, Scree, Second City, South Dakota Review, South Florida Poetry Journal, Steelhead, Story Quarterly, Today, TriQuarterly, Wisconsin Review* and *Wormwood Review*.

To David Pichaske

CONTENTS

from *GO READ THE RIVER*

The Hometown Hero Comes Home	3
Wedding Day	4
The Poet Dreams of His Youth	5
Bicycle	6
Invitation to a Young River Queen	7
Twisted Apples	8
Wind in the Tall Corn	9
Two Dreams of Kansas	10
December on the River	11
Short Stop	12
The Last Spring of an Old Family Name	13
Cicadas	14
As You Travel Ask Us	15
The Hitchhiker	16
Fourth of July	17
American Gothic	18
Two Beers in Argyle, Wisconsin	19
Hearts	20
Flight Pattern	21
The Midnight Fox	22
Illinois Pioneer's Diary: August 12, 1832	23
Theme in Yellow	24
In Guttenberg, Iowa	25
Romp	26
The Old Rail	27
Marbles	28
Drought Year	29
Grandma	30
After a Long Night in Keokuk	31
Moonflowers	32
Old Dubuque	33

Ghosts of Trains	34
From a Nineteenth-Century Kansas Painter's Notebook	35
The Girlie Magazines	36
Schoolhouse	37
Hollyhocks	38
Riverboat Shore Leave	39
Snow Country	40
Homesick in a River Town	41
Where I Am	42
Photographing a Nude	43
The Forgotten Graveyard	44
Hannibal, Missouri: Summer 1846	45
Thoreau	46
A House by the Tracks	47
Sun Dance Sun	48
Go Read the River	49
I and the Village	50

from THE LAST TRAIN TO PROPHETSTOWN

Land of Lincoln	53
On the Death of Adlai Stevenson	54
Light in August	55
At Sunset on the Prairie	56
Up the Illinois River	57
Central Standard Time	58
The Devil Comes to Ogle County	59
Country Graveyard	60
Noon at the Courthouse	61
Before the Tornado Tore Through Tazewell County	62
Warm	63
On the River at Savanna, Illinois	64
Porch Light	65
County Fair Images	66
Trumpet Above the Leaves	67

A Dark Night in Kane County	68
Great Northern	69
Evangelist	70
Folk Song for a Moonlit Banjo	71
You	72
RFD	73
The 7:23 to Chicago	74
Poor-White Blues Fisherman	75
The Fact	76
A Blond Tale	77
Grass	78
In the Mountains	79
Way Down in Arkansas	80
Iowa Gothic	81
On the Middle Border	82
Love Song	83
Are You Saying Me?	84
Thinking of Emily Dickinson at Bread Loaf, Vermont	85
Blue Leaves	86
Sometimes to East St. Louis	87
American Blues	88
In Time of Leaf Smoke	89
Three Hours After the Funeral of Aunt Jane I Try to Swing Like Sonny Rollins	90
Eldon's Circus	91
In Winter Sleep	92
Walking on the Great Plains	93
The Red Nude	94

from *STRAWBERRIES, VOYAGES TO THE INLAND SEA, CRABTREE'S WOMAN, WELL YOU NEEDN'T, BRIGHT MISSISSIPPI*

Chicken	97
Junkman's Spring	98
Two Days Out of Three Churches	99

Iowa Saturday Night	100
Phone Book Blues	101
One Dozen Valentines	102
Seen Aboard the *Texas Chief* During an Unscheduled Stop	103
Ask Me Now	104
Well You Needn't	105
Ruby, My Dear	106
I Mean You	107
Jackie-ing	108
In Walked Bud	109
Slow Train to Pittsburgh	110
The Porch	112
Bright Mississippi	113
A Farm in the Green Mountains	114

from CENTRAL STANDARD TIME, OPEN TO THE WIND, RIDING THE ROCK ISLAND THROUGH KANSAS, BOONDOCKS

Red Bricks	117
Poem on My Father's Eightieth Birthday	118
Barn Dreams	119
Long John Silver	120
Tumbleweeds	121
Old King Coal	122
Green-Eyed Boy After Reading Whitman and Sandburg	123
A Summer Tourist in Sorrento, Maine	124
Statement	125
Boondocks	126
The Ellsworth Brothers	127
That Old-Time Feeling	128
Home Cooking	129
Twenty Lines for Thomas Hart Benton	130
The Last Show in Tijuana	131
The Seventh Race at Lincoln, Nebraska	132

from *HOME STATE*

Courthouse Clocks	137
Scarecrow	138
Hambletonian	139
Tallgrass Prairie Plot	140
State Fair	141
Max	142
A Beardstown Dream	143
Chicago	144
Baseball	147
Dandelions	148
Populism	149
Hotel Nauvoo	150
Mail	151
Freight Trains	152
Screen Door	153
Three Poets	154
John Knoepfle	155
Pike County	156
Fishing	157
Sunflowers	158
Cornfields	159
Adlai Stevenson	160
Windmills	162
Some Smart Remarks on the Closing of the Hiram Walker Distillery in Peoria	163
Elizabeth Reed	164
Barns	165
Ignorance	166
Lust	167
Grant of Galena	168
Real Farmers	169
Cairo	170
Grandmother	171

Music	172
A Great Body	173
Olof Krans	174
Notes on Regionalism	175
Illinois River	176
Pipe Smoking	177
Fog	178
Bebop	179
Parade	180
Decatur	181
Alton's Giant	182
The Upper Crust	183
Rockford	184
Midwinter Thoughts	185
Catalpa	186
Lady Wrestler	187
Interstate 80	188
Barbershop	189
Doreen and God	190
Tough Luck in Quincy	191
Grain Elevator	192
Poetry Workshop	193
Goodbye	194

from *LIVE AT THE SILVER DOLLAR*

Failing	197
In Hoosier Dark	198
Black Sunflowers	200
Hot Summer Night in Central Illinois	201
The Railroad Wave	202
Stalking the Wild Wild River Roses	203
Trombone	204
Couple	205
House Party	206
Brass	207

The Main Event	208
Little Ruby	209
Green Dream	210
Bruise	211
Loose	212
Picasso	213
Apple Wine	214
Local Yokel	215
Chalk Lines	216
Burning Piano	217
Duluth	218
Tribute	219
Fourteen and a Half	220
Chicken-Fried Steak	221
The Stripper	222
Bluegrass Brothel	223
Cherokee Street	224
Drawing of a Happy Face	225
The Sandwich Fair	226
Charlie Parker	227
Aunt Alice Is Dead	228
A Bag of Seeds	229
Blue Margaritas	230
Young in Toledo	231
Dixie Truck Stop	232
Railroad Man	234
Limited	236
Daybreak in Another Town	237
Freckles	238
Live at the Silver Dollar	239
About the Author	240

*I don't know what other people are doing.
I just know about me.*

—Thelonious Monk

from
GO READ THE RIVER (1966)

*The river of your life flowed
from a more distant source than you suspected.
It rises still, a devious flood
between green banks of summer.
It is there forever,
tracing a prophecy across the earth.*

—Ross Lockridge, Jr., *Raintree County*

THE HOMETOWN HERO COMES HOME

This train, two Illinois counties late,
slips through jungles of corn and hot leaves
and the blazing helmets of huge barns.
My head spins with too much beer and sun
and the mixed feelings of going home.
The coach window has melted my face.
I itch where a birthmark darkens my skin.
The Jewish woman who sits next to me
sheds tears for a son, dead in Vietnam.
Her full lips are the color of crushed plums.
I want to go off with her to some lost
fishing village on the Mississippi
and be quiet among stones and small boats.
My fever breaks in the Galena hills.
It's too humid. No one will meet me.
And there are no brass bands in Dubuque.

WEDDING DAY

A blackbird sulks on the windowsill
where I have carved a dozen hearts.

I am in love with gin and sleep.

Between the long shadows of red barns
a strange girl calls me to a marriage
under honeysuckle strung with bees.

High in this cupola bedroom
I drift off in a bell of leaves.

Soon I will never be seen again.

THE POET DREAMS OF HIS YOUTH

The sad music of cello and bassoon.

The corn leaves are yellow.
I can never see them as green.

Sunflowers grow twenty feet tall
and stare the Bible from my eyes.

Hands that have burst their purple veins
float on the river where I was baptized.

In a tree of paper flowers
a calico girl makes valentines.

Every man, woman, and child of my youth
is standing by his own gravestone.

At dusk a boy with a red fish
comes out of the yellow corn leaves.

The sad music of cello and bassoon.

BICYCLE

Ever since he died
in a sports car
of a friend's friend
his old red
bicycle
that knew a paper route
has remained propped
against the screened porch
of the clapboard house
to rust with
alternate slants
of sun and rain
and this crabgrass end
of Cedar Street
is quiet for once
and the new boy
keeps the evening news
out of the tulip bed
but damn it all
I liked Phil Jones
who rests in peace
at the pine cone end
of Cedar Street
and why doesn't
someone put away
his old red
bicycle?

INVITATION TO A YOUNG RIVER QUEEN

Purple fish leap for the sun.

The sun is my crazy yellow hat
which I have tossed madly
into the girl-colored air.

I am quite beside myself with joy.

I love the fountains of grass
that spill over the river's edge.
I love worms and stones and bare toes.

You must come fishing with me.

You must come with your raintree sex,
your breasts of Easter eggs,
your thighs of taffy and moonflowers.

And you must wear your yellow hat.

TWISTED APPLES

Even the smashed
scarecrow
flaked out on
the tumbled fence
is not nearly
as grotesque
as these twisted
apples
that redden
the hard ground.
What puny
specimens.
What ruined flesh.
But also
what temptation
to try one,
to sink the teeth
down deep
and suck for juice,
then spit out
the small seeds
against the rude
and ruthless
weather.

WIND IN THE TALL CORN

A madcap wind bends back
the scarecrow's broomstick frame,
stumbles me slaphappy
down the Burlington track.
Strong gusts in the tall corn
set the tassels dancing.
Seven crows come to caw.
A girl with beefy thighs
wipes sweat off her red face,
then disappears in leaves.
Circus wind blows me wild
and woolly toward the house.
Beyond the railroad track
the scarecrow breaks his neck,
cries murder up his sleeve.

TWO DREAMS OF KANSAS

1

Forty-two grain elevators
have blown up
in Salina, Kansas.
I am buried in a loaf
of Sunbeam bread.

2

In a wheatfield,
west of Hays,
the fat thighs of a farm girl
are clamped around my loins.
I am dying of loneliness.

DECEMBER ON THE RIVER

In this overstuffed, bird-in-a-cage room,
the chipped keys of the player piano
are plinking out an old scrapbook tune.
I cannot call out its yellowed name.

Below Lock and Dam No. 11
they are dragging the Mississippi River
for the body of a deckhand from Epworth.

Stoned, leathered, and gimcracked with bad art,
our bluff house of blue lights chills my blood.

The player piano grinds to a quick stop.
All the bouncing keys are frozen stiff.

Snow begins to fall on Locust Street.

SHORT STOP

Then we stopped,
June sticky,
in Chillicothe,
Ohio,
to see my
jelly roll
girl cousin,
whose belly
shakes with fat
townships
of liquid laughter,
and after
sweet mountains
of sponge cake
and much beer,
we drove off
and I last saw her
blow me a kiss,
one for the road,
from the back porch
on her way
out back with
a big bag
of empties.

THE LAST SPRING OF AN OLD FAMILY NAME

A cardinal,
half-hidden
in oak leaves,

shakes out his bright
heritage
over this small

family plot
of gravestones
where I stare

at my own
remembered
roll call of names.

The cardinal,
his feathers
all slicked down,

flies away
to the green edge
of a cornfield

where I lose him
in the warm
red sunshine.

I return now
to muse among
these gravestones.

The proud names
bang in my ears
like screen doors.

And I am loved
in a hundred
springtime places.

CICADAS

After
a long rain

sun-stung
cicadas

with bright
onion skin

wings
razor

the heavy
yellow air

to wiry
shrillness

and red-eyed
summer

climbs
back to love

twanging
ragtime

AS YOU TRAVEL ASK US

*On the left the Saxby home. There are four Saxby
boys, all of whom can move their ears.*

—George Ade, *The Tortures of Touring*

And these kids can
move their asses too,
especially after
letting a car have it
with a few tomatoes.
I've seen them do it.
Splat, splat, splat, splat.
Four ripe ones smack
some old codger's Chevy,
and before Granddad
knows what happened
these rascals vanish
and laugh to beat hell
all the way back home,
where under the elms
they roll around like dogs
gone mad with fleas.

THE HITCHHIKER

When farmers in Fords
won't even stop,
and you're famished,
and you know your girl
paces up and down
on the cold veranda
of her windy house
in Oskaloosa,
bluing the blue air with
"Where's that damn boy?
He's always late,"
there are always rocks
to throw at billboards
pushing Jesus,
Elsie the Borden Cow,
Holiday Inn,
and the Green Giant.

Smack 'em real good,
right between the eyes.

That's the way to go.

FOURTH OF JULY

Under
a speech
making
at the courthouse
sun
yippee boys
Yankee Doodle
the flag
waving
weather
with their toy
drums
and firecrackers
spoil the games
of little girls
who scoop up
candy
colored
balls and jacks
to run away
in full retreat
flanked by troops
and jeered by
J
P
Sousa

AMERICAN GOTHIC

Smoky autumn
straight shots
of amber sun
pour through
the tangled
park elm trees
where bent
old men sit
to talk about
the railroads
and muse
on that last
precious fourth
of a fifth
of Old Crow
buried deep
among frayed
shirts across
the IC tracks
and why can't
Charlie Potts
remember
to bring along
his dad-blamed
hip flask?

TWO BEERS IN ARGYLE, WISCONSIN

Birds fly in the broken windows
of the hotel in Argyle.
Their wings are the cobwebs
of abandoned lead mines.

Across the street at Skelly's
the screen door bangs against the bricks
and the card games last all day.

Another beer truck comes to town,
chased by a dog on three legs.

Batman lies drunk in the weeds.

HEARTS

This you must know:
The pretty girl
with the spring-wind hair,
who has carved hearts
on every single
sycamore tree,
is not in love with you,
is not even in love.
But she found this knife
which has a long,
wicked cutting edge.
You see how it is, boy?
And she must make her mark,
must dig into the sap,
the warm flesh of life,
to touch and cut and shape.
This you must know.

FLIGHT PATTERN

The brown paper
airplane
looped once,
looped twice,
then dove
smack-dab into
a flower bed
of four-o'clocks.
The boy was damn tired
of watching only
two little loops
then *kerplunk,*
so butchered
the brown paper
airplane
with his jackknife.
This put a bad crimp
in the big plans
to make Jasper Street
an important
air center.
Later, his aunt
said it was
the awful heat
and especially
the aroma
of four-o'clocks
that did it.

THE MIDNIGHT FOX

Through fields of ragged corn
the midnight fox
wears a moon on his back,
but still eludes
on weary legs
the pack of yelping dogs.
Now the grim-faced hunter,
blister-sore in new boots,
blasts off his shotgun twice.
A corn ear smacks the ground.
The moon turns fox.

ILLINOIS PIONEER'S DIARY: AUGUST 12, 1832

After my vexing, dull chores were done,
and surrounded by baskets of corn,
I sang under the summer oak trees,
going over and over again
the sad hymns we sing so loud in church.

Then turning to poetry and Burns,
I recited to the frogs and bees,
Pa's favorite, "Man Was Made to Mourn."
The words melted in fevers of sun,
and I was wedded to trees and corn.

THEME IN YELLOW

A cold wind from Waterloo
loosens the yellow apples.
They fall in the front yard and roll
to where an old willow tree
breathes through her thin hair.
The streetlamp lights up
a girl's yellow hair ribbon.
My mother died in a yellow nightgown.
It sweeps the worn kitchen floor
on windy, sleepless nights.

IN GUTTENBERG, IOWA

In a shady side yard
in Guttenberg, Iowa,
find not Mark Twain
in a white linen suit,
but Big Ed Muehlebach,
who sits there smoking,
an old steamboat pilot dreaming
with his lazy collie dog
by a lacy willow tree,
while a freight train shakes
down to river-sucked Dubuque
under high bluffs turned
to a child's book of color.
Now Big Ed Muehlebach,
neat in his white linen suit,
watches a towboat push upriver
eight barges filled with coal,
after locking through
Lock and Dam No. 10.
And Big Ed Muehlebach
never thought of Mark Twain
on his long, gull-blown stretch
on the Mississippi.

ROMP

Her
strong
white
legs
are
wet
grass
stained
I
help
her
up
she
grabs
my
neck
rubs
cool
milk-
weed
in
my
hot
face
and
I
am
glad
she
chose
to
run

THE OLD RAIL

Again the old rail,
my uncle Chandler,
brings us lumps of coal
and big brass buttons
in a brakeman's cap.

From the rusty
cemetery of trains
he brings us the M&StL
and the Iowa Central
in a battered caboose.

In a timetable suit
he comes to this town
of silent tracks
and lost spur lines,
yelling "Highball!"

And then he talks of
the Kate Shelley bridge,
Mikado type locomotives,
and mile-long freights
to Eagle Grove.

MARBLES

Now ten years old,
he carries
a big leather
bag of marbles
down his home block,
slouching with
its rock weight,
to a match game
with the champ
of Maple Street,
and what great hopes
will roll with
that favorite
blue-green agate,
there in the smooth
circle of dirt
by the pear tree.

DROUGHT YEAR

The high-tension lines
string up the western sun.
Near the city limits sign,
black with bullet holes,
a lean wind fools
in the cottonwoods
and a single cornstalk
rattles its yellow teeth
under the slow drift
of a buzzard's cloud.
Off the sticky blacktop
tumbled gravestones
whisper of burning barns
and the fevered brows
of heatstroked children.
In a weedy creekbed
the whiskey bottle
has a sun devil's eye.

GRANDMA

A sweet pea
stuck in each
grass-stained ear
sneaks up barefoot
behind
soapsuds Grandma
with a dead-fly
flyswatter
swats her topknot
hard hard hard
take that
for not frying
doughnuts
you promised me
and that
for not telling
about
Jesse James
and this
for being so
old old old

AFTER A LONG NIGHT IN KEOKUK

Morning,
pale as a fish,
slips inside
and rooftops
spin away
to a forest
of burnt corn
and birdsong
shrivels up
the leaves
in the round
Grant Wood trees.
We lie here
in bed
in a motel
in Keokuk,
Iowa,
and we got gin
and we got smokes
and we got your
sad childhood
to talk about,
and mine too.
And I refuse
to answer
the phone
or the knuckles
on our door.

MOONFLOWERS

River roads of insects
rub summer in the ears
of slow farmers.

In the sweet crotch
of a sassafras tree
Janet sucks hard candy
and jabs brown toes
at her little brother.

A wind out of Kansas
carries rumors
of wild wheat fires
and the blue eyes
of young soldiers.

Near the screen door
moonflowers bloom:
shy faces of farm girls.

OLD DUBUQUE

*There is no past, present and future time
here in Dubuque, there is just Dubuque time.*
—Richard Bissell

From Grant's grave Galena
we drove down in a daze,
from two days of antiques,
to the Mississippi,
then crossed over at noon
to old, hunchbacked Dubuque,
a never-say-die town,
a gray, musty pawnshop
still doing business, while
on the bluff, blue jeans flapped
in a river wind laced
with fresh paint and dead carp.

We couldn't find the house
where she once lived and died,
at ninety, baking bread,
somewhere in the hard maze
of crusty shops and streets,
and Dubuque is a spry,
goofy-sad river gal,
lost in a patchwork haze
of tears and years gone by,
and I love this mad place
like my dead grandmother
loved her steins of Star beer.

GHOSTS OF TRAINS

By the forgotten railroad tracks
summer weeds grow tall as Lincoln.
We lie here in thick yellow weeds.
We talk. The heat shapes our love words.
Ghosts of trains. Whistles in the night.
Sounds of love, crossed with youth and pain.
Trains bound for Denver, Chicago,
trains we lost in lonely cornfields.
I rest my head on your moist thighs.
Your big breasts coax my passion up.
It is strange we should meet again.
My loins ache. The hot night breathes hard.

FROM A NINETEENTH-CENTURY KANSAS PAINTER'S NOTEBOOK

I always paint
pictures
of violent weather,
mostly tornadoes
with thick dragon tails
that strike like death,
then give them away
to queasy aunts
and quaking uncles.
Though I find peace
in strawberry sunsets
and those May wine days
when a clover breeze
ding-dongs the tulips,
I am obsessed
with steep
funnel-shaped clouds
and frightened children
who cry and run scared
through towering
summer cornfields.
I paint only
the dark-stained
pictures
that storm in my head.

THE GIRLIE MAGAZINES

Ah, here they are.

Pink taffy
nipples
top breasts
too creamy,
too perfect.
There is no
female
who has steep hills
of flesh
like this blonde.
Only from
the skilled use
of a brush
and wet dream
of an artist
too much alone
could this
nude come forth
to stand here
between pages 12
and 14
of a sex mag.

I'll buy this one.

SCHOOLHOUSE

The fat sun of midday
churned our milky brains
to buttermilk
as we laughed and war whooped
through Roy Goodenow's
cornfield
on our way to toss stones
at the abandoned
one-room schoolhouse.

After the first smash
of brittle glass
we drew near to find
the chalky ghost
of old Miss Krause
writing in bat blood
fifteen-letter words,
at least five feet high,
on the dusty blackboard.

Cicadas sang
beyond sycamore trees,
a corn wind blew red dust
in eyes that had blinked
at too much sun,
and when Jack pulled the bell
we all ran away
through Roy Goodenow's
cornfield.

HOLLYHOCKS

Hollyhocks are swaying gently
under the blue branches of an elm.
I watch eighty-two freight cars
sink into the corn leaves
and drop over the rim of the prairie.
On my back now, I watch white clouds
make wool pictures of mothers.
Two blackbirds fly toward the river,
the muddy river of endless regret.
I could lie here forever
and look up at these hollyhocks.
I will never get on in the world.

RIVERBOAT SHORE LEAVE

This old county seat town,
caged in a jungle of corn,
contains thirteen beer bars
with the usual wide
selection of nuts,
one pigeoned railroad station
on the Rock Island Line,
one sweaty-eyed courthouse clock,
and, most significant,
one buggy screen door
that I can knock on,
then stagger inside
to a cucumber sandwich
and a cold bottle of Grain Belt,
and there is always
a fooling around session
with Penelope Jane,
after Uncle Max
takes off for a game of pool
or a round of golf,
which often leads to
a mammoth four-poster bed,
where three people have died
in their damp summer sleep
from too much summer heat,
and sex was never blamed.

SNOW COUNTRY

Only
a little
yellow

school bus
creeping along
a thin

ribbon
of snow road
splashed color

on the white
winter canvas
that was

Wyoming
from the train
yesterday

HOMESICK IN A RIVER TOWN

In the valley of the Wapsipinicon,
schoolgirls are picking leaves off old trees,
autumn ambushed in a wagon wheel woods.

I am cold and homesick in this river town.

All morning I sat by the Indian water
and dreamed among weeds and sleeping willows.

Now I wander in the woods of my lost youth
to hear the carousel laughter of girls.

My eyes want the backyard faces of trees.
My hands ache for familiar touch and feel.

The wind comes up. I am drowning in leaves.

I am spinning away on a dead maple leaf.
I am rolling down the hill of boyhood
to this red-brick town I cannot love.

WHERE I AM

My wife draws a scarlet kangaroo
where once we hung Toulouse-Lautrec.

The baby dreams in her crib of eyes
and runs from Humpty Dumpty.

Beyond the crawling tomato vines
an owl digs my grave on the moon.

PHOTOGRAPHING A NUDE

She faces
the strong sun
from a kneeling
position
her small head
thrown back
to remove
a blue shadow
that was brushing
her full lips
her pear-shaped
breasts
hang down
like sun-burst
fruit
and amber
summer grass
rises up
to tickle
the dark hairs
on her tan
forearms
she poses
with patience
known only
to camels
and Chinese
philosophers
while across
the stony field
two beavers
soak their tails
in creek water

THE FORGOTTEN GRAVEYARD

I have left my townsmen down below
under the shadows of Town Hall:
religious fakers, Republicans,
the windbags at the barbershop.

On this hill, the clean smell of skunk.

The ape-faced trees crouch like gnarled bootblacks
over the yellowed tombstones,
and there is a bird's nest—a torn blue wig.

But I am at home among the dead,
the deformed, the discolored.

A woodpecker joyfully carves his hole.

The sunset sweetens the mouth of a leaf.

HANNIBAL, MISSOURI: SUMMER 1846

Today's last riverboat has come, with cheers, and gone,
and Hannibal, Missouri, settles down again,
sweat-soaked, dog-day groggy in the fierce summer sun.
Dusty roads are almost deserted to pink pigs
that grub and snort among last evening's melon rinds.
Water Street clerks, tired of talk about city girls,
throw away cigars and tilt back split-bottom chairs
to drowse and dream through their river-lapped reveries.
The town drunkard and a stringbean, motherless youth,
who is learning the wayward ways of whiskey,
are fish-deep in sleep on the small stone-fisted wharf.
High up on the hill, under the town's damp green leaves,
a huckleberry pie cools on a windowsill,
while beyond the jail and John Clemens's whitewashed fence,
the wild, river-eyed boys tie up their "Injun Joe."

THOREAU

Summer: hillsides of ripe huckleberries
just short minutes from Concord's busy hub.
Bored with Emerson's transcendental talk,
he plucks perfect fruit off a hearty shrub.

Happy he chose this green road not taken,
he squeezes the firm flesh of his desire,
loving the warm purple juice, forsaken
until he stretched forth his cool hand of fire.

A HOUSE BY THE TRACKS

Snow falls, stops, starts again.
Santa Fe, Wabash, Seaboard.
The freight train earth cracks in two.
Nickel Plate, Nickel Plate.
There are curses on the courthouse wind.
B&O, L&N.
South of town, a farmer has been shot
by a hunter with a Jim Beam face.
Illinois Central, Illinois Central,
Frisco, Atlantic Coast Line,
Great Northern, Great Northern,
Pennsylvania, Rock Island.
Cops are burning up the county roads.
Missouri Pacific.
The black branches of mulberry trees
are writing my name on the backs of barns.
Union Pacific, Norfolk and Western,
Burlington, Soo Line, Burlington.
I have hot coffee on the stove
and fresh doughnuts from the A&P.
B&O, L&N,
Milwaukee Road, Nickel Plate,
Santa Fe, Boston and Maine.
I have never been so all alone, so
Erie-Lackawanna.

SUN DANCE SUN

Sun dance sun
Apache brazen
Shoshone bold

war dance sun
war paint bright
assaults the cold

swift sassy
brave brassy
arrows of sun

bleed the day
to a tomahawked
scarlet death

in the crisp
Indian summer
afternoon

GO READ THE RIVER

This little brick town
by the Mississippi
never did see
its prettiest schoolgirls
run around naked
in hollyhock yards
or hear a band
that could play good Dixie,
but that isn't why
the place went to pot,
why the sun-bleached shades
are drawn on Main Street,
or why the slowest trains
thunder by now
to blow thick dust
against the beer signs.

I AND THE VILLAGE

I will wear my best green face
and put on a strawberry hat.
Today I will turn this town
upside down and inside out.
I will stop and sing the old songs
at the houses of my townsmen:
yellow houses, lavender houses,
houses with chickens and uncles,
houses with hunchbacks and apples.
Today I will kiss all the farm girls
and play my silver violin
on the marble steps of the courthouse.
And I will tip my strawberry hat
to every green face I see.

from

THE LAST TRAIN TO PROPHETSTOWN (1968)

Back of Chicago the open fields—were you ever there?
Trains coming toward you out of the West—
Streaks of light on the long gray plains?—many a song
Aching to sing.

—Sherwood Anderson, *Mid-American Chants*

LAND OF LINCOLN

Rain that falls at blistering noon
steams the cracked hides of battered barns.
Today the whole state of Illinois
is sticky with tree sap and spit of sun.
A woman with three tattered shopping bags
climbs out of the town auto dump
and hobbles past the smashed school bus
that is rusting away behind half a Chevrolet.
Beyond the boarded-up church,
a windmill has a face of broken bones.
Suddenly depressed, I brood upon
the ruins of Mormon homes in Nauvoo
and the blasted skulls of steamboats
left sightless in weeds near Grafton.
And where is the last train to Prophetstown?
Has it, too, felt the heavy hand of history?
Yes, scars on the startled landscape of Illinois.
But there have been terrible man-scars also:
Elijah Lovejoy murdered by a mob in Alton.
Joseph Smith murdered by a mob in Carthage.
Negroes murdered by a mob in Springfield.
Lindsay gone. Masters gone. Sandburg gone.
Abe gone. Darrow gone. Altgeld the Eagle gone.
Little Giant Douglas gone. Stevenson gone.
Friends, I got the weary blues,
and these sunflowers bent to gravestones
push me to dreams of sullen sleep.
But wait. Hold on. Look over there.
Some boys are building a new tree house.
Strong and clear-eyed and trusting they are.
I stand taller and walk to that chosen oak,
its leaves bouncing with hammered joy.
Okay. Enough. Right here. Now.
I will begin to move among the living again.

ON THE DEATH OF ADLAI STEVENSON

Night comes before we know it.
Watching the fireflies in the front yard,
an Illinois farmer licks salt-dry lips.
The darkness surrounds all glowing things.
We want to hold the hands we love forever.
Long freight trains drum-roll their prairie rails.
On the slow river of an oak leaf
a brave heart winks out.

LIGHT IN AUGUST

Home once more under the dying elms,
I watch gnats bug the last slants of rusty sun.
This wicker chair eases my traveling bones.
The funeral sermon would have peeved you, Grandpa,
for you didn't cotton to a man who gushed.
I recall those boyhood visits to the country:
the wide wraparound porch, the creaking windmill,
and at dusk the corn leaves flapped green wings.
When August swelters, I will think of chicken dinners
and the night ball games at Clinton.
Also, there were always surprises in the attic,
and in the barn, and among the put-up beans.
"Study closely the small, quiet things," you said.
Again I see bright kernels of Indian corn,
cabbage butterflies, wrinkled apples, lumps of coal,
and all those lost Burna-Shave signs.
No, Grandpa, I will not forget the hill farm,
nor your pride in state and special place.
Damn, eighty-eight Bill Goodenow summers,
and you never stopped talking about Lincoln.

AT SUNSET ON THE PRAIRIE

At sunset on the prairie,
great cornfields climb to the sky.
My sunburned arms are sticky with sweat
and sprinkled with pollen.
There are sad mouths in the shadows
that hunger to be kissed.
I watch the last streaks of pink light
fade beyond the water tower.
In the kitchen of tall windows
a moon girl sings my name.
Oh what dark secrets I have gathered
to amaze her flashing eyes.

UP THE ILLINOIS RIVER

Ragged leaves and cigar wrappers
scurry across the beaten grass.
The river waters my dusty eyes.
Stray-dog sunlight tongues a pale petal
that is shaped like a gambler's hand.
Thunder booms in the west
and all the sailing clouds come home.
Drops of rain fall, big as walnuts.
Ghosts of drowned deckhands
talk about coal and jinxed towboats,
then lie back, quiet, exhausted
in their castles of catfish.
Off to the south, a feather of smoke:
an Illini girl burns her wedding dress.
Twilight comes, slime-green and eerie.
Now the air is soft, belly smooth.
The boy who moves out of the lamplight
has a guitar as big as God.
If he plunks just one taut string,
I will explode a thousand images.

CENTRAL STANDARD TIME

1

Under a plum tree,
a battered kitchen chair,
painted a swamp-frog green,
over the blue, over the cream,
shows off a roly-poly lady,
just in from Carbondale,
who fans between hot legs
with *Good Housekeeping.*

2

The closet shelves are stacked
with *Wall Street Journal*s.
I find a book by Eddie Guest.
I hear the UN damned.
Well, they warned me:
"You'll be the first poet here
since Vachel Lindsay
took the wrong train to Vandalia."
My refrigerator shudders
under the insurance calendar.

3

In paleface Old Shawneetown,
standing among the fish heads,
the Argo Corn Starch Indian
steps out of a shiny cob body
and whispers in my ear,
"They all went thataway."

THE DEVIL COMES TO OGLE COUNTY

The rustle of skeleton weeds
at the river of slow trickle
muffled just snatches
of his thick Missouri drawl.
Yes, it's this preacher I'm talking about,
this Elmer Gantry in a seersucker suit
who slammed out of a lamb-white Chrysler
as if he had to maybe take a leak
against the twisted willow,
but instead began shouting
Numbers and Deuteronomy.

If he was rehearsing there
for the big bad sinners
of Ogle County,
I,
queasy in the milk-sick sun,
was his only congregation,
leastways
no one else
scampered up the hill
when he rolled a perfect skull
from a crimson bandanna.

COUNTRY GRAVEYARD

Cows with eyes of buttered moons
doze along the barbed wire.
Weeds grow to impossible heights.
I call out my family names
across the campsites of stones:
Etter, Wakefield, McFee, Goodenow.
Cedar trees shake fat crows
from their ragged beards.
In the farmhouse, back from the road,
shades are drawn against noon sun
and grace is said before the meat.
I stand among these gravestones
where a wet-nosed wind coughs
gray dust on my pinching shoes.
The rusty bells of the brick church.
Goodenow, McFee, Wakefield, Etter.

NOON AT THE COURTHOUSE

This brick courthouse is whiskey faced.
Look at all the red old granddads.

What rube drew a judge on the john wall,
then blacked him in real good?

Across the street at the Hotel Tall Corn
the witness circles a glass of milk.

Loud barbers say Ben's case is lost now
and the Negro might just maybe hang.

A farmer stuffed in pig-shit boots
squeaks down the marble stairs.

The lawyer lights one more White Owl
and jabbers away about Clarence Darrow.

Out here on the lawn, dead county leaves
are crumpled parking tickets.

Propped up by the town's Honor Roll,
I fall asleep over an apple core.

BEFORE THE TORNADO TORE THROUGH TAZEWELL COUNTY

Beyond the senior high school
the sky is a watery melon-rind green.

Listen to the new corn breathe.

My uncle is looking for leaf holes
and singing "Skip to My Lou."

Not a spear of grass is dancing.

How can I read *Gone with the Wind*
when the blind dog barks?

Burlington: "Way of the Zephyrs."

Cherry boughs turn blackbird
and huge clouds suck up the sun.

Something bugs me. I got an itch.

WARM

A stiff breeze plays among the corn tassels.
Milky juice thickens in the corn ears.
Half-awake, I realize with a start
that it is really Ann Rutledge I love.
Here in Illinois the fat earth is breathing deeply
and I know nothing but lazy lustfulness.
Slim Ann Rutledge of lost New Salem
had blue eyes and long auburn hair.
You can walk through a cornfield at dusk and see Lincoln.
The leaves rustle there and a tall man grieves.
Ann Rutledge is a spun dream of purple corn silk
drifting over this hammock of summer thighs.
When the prairie moon returns, I shall sleep again,
wrapped in the rags of a husk-brown coat.

ON THE RIVER AT SAVANNA, ILLINOIS

A blonde girl who looks like Doris Day
is sweeping cigar butts and dead bees
off a Sunday porch of busted chairs.
Foamy waves push inside my skull
where I keep those get-acquainted jokes
and quips to use on shy natives.
Two hours and twenty-six minutes late,
the Chicago train stops at the depot.
All the passengers swallow their watches.
I lean over the whiskers of a catfish
and whistle three bars of "Summertime."
A coin of rain falls on the Comics.
The train limps out of town, discouraged,
thoroughly whipped, done for.

PORCH LIGHT

My pipe smoke drifts to the porch light.
I have stepped outside to call the cat,
who is walking a picket fence of old moons.
A sooty mist is falling on
grape leaves, two rows of sweet corn,
and the boards of our storm cellar door.
A string of cars pulls out of the station:
the last shabby train back to childhood.
I grew up in a morning-glory town
under a cathedral of giant elms,
a carefree banger of screen doors,
a smug loafer and laugh getter
on all the gingerbread porches.
Then Mother went mad one hullabaloo day
on a hillside of black-eyed susans,
Chicago, Hartford, Topeka.
Doctors, doctors, doctors.
And throughout all the ticking gone time,
though I hated the very damn sight of it,
I would let no one touch her violin.
Oh, the Devil stares with a thousand eyes
and screams in the unstrung flowers.
Above the porch light, crusty with bugs,
grape leaves rattle in a damp wind.

COUNTY FAIR IMAGES

Ten kewpie dolls are primping
behind a house of pigs.

Snorting in the popcorn dust,
gigantic new corn pickers
frighten all one-arm farmers.

The blue-ribbon Jersey bull
is running for county sheriff.

On the dizzy merry-go-round
a dwarf in pickle-green shorts
feeds his horse a chocolate egg.

These Sandy Flemish rabbits
look like loaves of bread rising.

The winning sulky driver
is a polka-dot clown,
drowning in a smile of roses.

TRUMPET ABOVE THE LEAVES

I stand on the roof of my gusty house
in a golden-booted fall wind.
Slouching in brown windbreakers,
the boys of Kane Street kick leaves
to windy congregations on grass
that tangles in a net of toys.
The wild horse of my grand roof
can ride any man bell over steeple.
If you want to tell your townsmen
fall is here with a blast of horn,
go up above skittery leaves, I tell you.
A roller derby of plump pumpkins
bumps down steps, scattering cats.
My old shiny-new trumpet never sounded
better and better and better.
Hell, I know what I'm doing, kid.

A DARK NIGHT IN KANE COUNTY

The headlight of a westbound freight train
moves restlessly back and forth.

Having run with a crowd of ragged clouds,
the moon sulks in its cave of dead stars.

There are scavenger eyes in cornfields.

A wailing diesel horn late at night
is the desperate plea of a runaway boy,
one hour skipped out from reform school.

All the doors are locked on State Street.

The smooth, delicate hands of my townsmen
are digging in private gardens of guilt.

In the cemetery, leaves drop on wet grass.
A size twelve boot kicks at a tall headstone.

GREAT NORTHERN

1

What is it about a Great Northern boxcar,
standing on a cold siding in Minneapolis,
that fills me with such nameless joy?

2

Wave, boy, that's *The Winnipeg Limited*!

3

Inarticulate, lacking paper words,
I celebrate the railroads in my blood.

4

Have you ever ridden *The Western Star*?

5

Through the snowfields of central Minnesota
The Empire Builder plunges into the night,
and I shake by the thundering tracks,
crying hoarsely: "Love, love, love."

6

Trains, the beautiful, goddamn trains.

EVANGELIST

Take my right hand
yes my right hand
plant it as seed
then let rain fall
and let sun fall
celebrate this day
run the red dogs
through the streets
of your sullen towns
through the farms
wasting away with
corn corn corn
and nervous with
the caw caw of crows

A new day comes
is coming has come
beans beans beans
we want no beans
blow some brassy
money marches
arise you hicks
husks of Lincoln
take my right hand
plant it as seed
then stand you back
and watch me work
for Jesus Christ
and Illinois

FOLK SONG FOR A MOONLIT BANJO

Oh, it's Quincy, Alton, Cairo,
down the long river road we go.

Green green greener, the leaves flash by
like promises, like tongues dancing.

Find the weasel. Find the drifter.
Find the river blessed with girls.

High on a hill of willow hearts
pink blossoms ooze their shy perfume.

Go now, spread out blankets of blue fog
to close those fierce sinners in.

Moon water slips past a strangled Jill,
a jack of clubs, a jug of corn.

Soon the mouths of grief and hate.
Soon the questions scorched with fear.

Old whippoorwill knows, and the grass,
and the brown farmer knocked to dreams.

YOU

You?
Good god, golden girl,
I thought of you in eerie-laked Cleveland,
expiring among the taxicabs and Shell stations.
And I thought of you in Bowling Green, Ohio,
belching a third Royal Crown Cola
in my Best Western motel pajamas.
And I thought of you in Goshen, Indiana,
rubbernecking the Amish and the Mennonites.
And now back home in the Land of Lincoln,
I think of you again and again and again
while washing up with American Family soap,
after a fun-filled day at Acme Brake-Shoe.
You!

RFD

For luck, I stick wet chicory
inside my denim shirt.

Drizzle turns to hard rain
as I slam shut
the wobbly mailbox.

There is no hope, I see.
Wilma will not write.

On the screened porch
I juggle three bruised
Winesap apples.

The sun tries but just can't make it.

I rock in the swing
and think of snowfall
on rutted county roads.

A loose shutter bangs
behind my eyes.

Now all the maple trees
roll on the grass
and burn scarlet.

And it's blues October again
at Penny Whistle Farm.

THE 7:23 TO CHICAGO

Another train from the bedroom towns
crams through iron jaws of the shed.

Stooped commuters with paper hearts
jiggle their dull and dollar eyes.

Stone-fisted towers wear smoke hats
and cough in the faces of bank clerks.

And I, nagged into a reg-u-lar job,
hear pool balls clicking in my head.

POOR-WHITE BLUES FISHERMAN

Muddy water lap and suck and ooze.
Oh, Sherwood, you poor-white bastard me,
it's snail lonesome here, old blues man,
so gloomy in this sad country town.
Big fish he bite, fish he slip away.
And that sun, that Pike County sun,
it sure jumps the Jack-climbing corn,
but whoooo-eee, it prickles my groin
and sticks my hair and swims my skin.
Waiting, yes, I'm still waiting here.
I'm surely not going no place now,
for it's this lazy brown-woman stream
I aim to make high-summer love to,
this river with her squirming thighs.
Ah, come up, cat, come up, you fish face.

THE FACT

The going-home sun
smiles my railroad eyes.
I run a rough stick
across the last picket fence.
Under our tulip tree
you wait in the yellow dust,
smoothing a lilac dress.
I touch my arms, my chest,
watch my moving feet.
I have to know it's me,
really me, always me.

A BLOND TALE

They started teaching algebra an' I didn't give
a goddam what X stood for so I quit.
—Tennessee Williams, *This Property Is Condemned*

I awake from a long afternoon nap
to hear strange names in the shadows,
a blond tale told by a bluejay.
Deep, deep the sour waters of my skull.
The dusty sun sews purple leaves
on the pulled-down windowshade
and a branch holds out trembling fingers.
A circus of numbers. Round and round.
My December wife dances in a white dress
under a 100-year-old elm tree
and wonders what happened to Mary Jane.
My answers? Answers? What answers?
The leaves are wandering children
whose names are chalked on blackboards
of a schoolhouse choked now with weeds.
All right, where am I? Where is my name?
Did I go too soon? Am I gone forever?
A chilly wind comes to erase the sun.
The bluejay tells no more stories.

GRASS

The spring grass is growing tall
where the hearty sun shines.

There are green worlds in the grass,
gatherings of laughing men.

There is hope in the grass,
and I found innocence there.

In the eye of a grass field
my son waves his blond arms.

I wave back and churn toward him,
the thick grass around my thighs.

Grass in the dawn of a new day
smells of rivers and clean flesh.

Oh, to be born on prairie grass.
Oh, to romp in the leaves of love.

IN THE MOUNTAINS

I have been here before.

The same pinched child or smudged dwarf
falls out of a mockernut tree
to plop beside me on the smoke-blue grass.

Yes, I remember. Yes. Sure.

Under the cracked ribs of the porch,
the bootlegger's boy, in love with rivers,
blows steamboats out of a Nehi bottle.

Nothing's changed. Nothing.

Now the ghosts of American revolutionaries
take my hat, my bags, my money
and stammer in Elizabethan.

Well, it's been a long, long time.

So glad to see me, the old woman
sticks out the longest tongue in all Kentucky.
We laugh, plucking our yellowed hearts.

WAY DOWN IN ARKANSAS

At my aunt Roberta's,
a bronze eagle flies over the door.
On the tip-and-turn table,
a big wooden bowl of Osage oranges,
a magnifying glass,
and an ashtray from Antoine's.
Uncle Herb clowns in an oval frame.
In the stuffy back parlor,
wallpaper of pale yellow roses
and a white cat on the sofa.
The side yard is walnut trees.
If I should go there again,
she would give me shepherd's pie
and a patchwork quilt.
And I would be pacing the porch,
smoking a cob pipe,
then walking down to the drugstore
to look over the high school girls.
Maybe October. Maybe not.
Maybe never, Aunt Roberta.

IOWA GOTHIC

Rude wind is picking the rusty locks
of all abandoned one-room schoolhouses.

A church bell, taken from a wrecked steamboat,
tolls no more across the fox-blood hills.

Antique light under wilting corn leaves
holds strange secrets and forgotten promises.

In the ballpark where I played third base
a billy goat fouls the infield grass.

My boyhood home is where the Moose meet.
Only the bar is open at Brown's Hotel.

Mary, the girl I married, then lost,
sells scrapbooks at the Ben Franklin store.

The last passenger train to Waterloo
sports a roaming eye that can drive men wild.

Prairie stars. Full moon. Deep purple sky.
Night birds, find me a new place to stand.

ON THE MIDDLE BORDER

Six grackles on the blue lawn
strut around like sailors.

All country roads in these parts
lead to houses with great doors.

Love the fat, freckled children
hidden in the dark elms.

Lavender flowers. Lavender.
Brood now on lavender.

Josie, Josie, my lost angel,
I've come to make you my wife.

A sudden storm of wild boys
moves toward doors and lilacs.

Ship-tall and dusted with stars,
I'm set to fun or fight.

LOVE SONG

Just because I stick a scarlet maple leaf
in your pale hair
is certainly no guarantee
you will burn sweetly
with the season's ripe passion
or even warm to my touch

but

your smile comes on now
gently glowing gladly
and the slow blood of nineteen Wisconsin autumns
rises in your cool apple cheeks
and your lazy arms leap up
and your quiet breasts speak of love

and

suddenly there is real round red joy
here in spinning October
as our private woods
blaze out brightly
into great heart pounding
hallelujahs

ARE YOU SAYING ME?

I'm winded on a Cyclone fence.
Do your ears like to run away?

Ohio is hill and back.
Just follow the yellow brick road.

Buttermilk drinks spooky.
I want a gingerbread witch.

Goblins are owls with funny shoes.
Black cat has lost his question.

My rocking horse coughs bad breath.
Do we kiss the garbage man?

Larry is laughing roses.
I live in a house of long tongues.

It's cold under a curly leaf.
Wrap me up a Navaho.

Dogs wink when their tails are tired.
I'm dead in my red head.

THINKING OF EMILY DICKINSON
AT BREAD LOAF, VERMONT

Walking this morning through the forest,
cool and damp and sweet with rot,
I find red and yellow mushrooms
that are soft and rubbery to my touch,
and I find silver-speckled stones
stuck in sand by the skipping stream,
and I find the skin of a birch tree
hanging loose and curly from the trunk,
and on a stump in a flower of sun
I find a toad no bigger than my eye,
and I think of you now, Emily,
knowing that you in your sure-footed joy
would know what secrets are revealed here
by mushroom, stone, birch bark, toad.
Yours was the harvest of small mysteries.

BLUE LEAVES

She stands in the front yard.
Leaves fall on her brown hair
and leaves touch her knees
and her dress is blue.

Blue, my color of remembrance.

I stand in the front yard.
Leaves fall on my bald head
and my knees are birds
and brown leaves burn blue.

Blue, my color of remembrance.

SOMETIMES TO EAST ST. LOUIS

Yes, we are to East St. Louis,
'cause Cousin Kate called us last night.
Said, "Come over here and play guitar."

My girl cousins are all man-crazy.
One tried to go Merchant Marine
and, you know, she damn near made it.

You play a little guitar jazz
and watch old Mississippi slide past
and you want to go bye bye too.

My hot cousin Kate called us last night
and we are to East St. Louis
to diddle around and drink it up.

Sure, I'll have another. You buyin', K?

AMERICAN BLUES

The wind tumbles blue-eyed wildflowers
against new headstones in wheat towns.

Young boys clutch baseballs and marbles
and puzzle over their fathers' graves.

The long limbs of American soldiers
grow cold in the torn mouths of swamps.

No angel looks homeward.

IN TIME OF LEAF SMOKE

Trees are dropping their alphabets.
We must spell out the loves we have lost.
I fumble around picking up letters.
The grass is thick with old girlfriends.
What is your first name again?
A town of silent faces slips through the sun.
This smoky light confuses my eyes.
I see noses, blowing hair, ears.
I'll use some reds and some yellows.
Well, I can't find a C or a T.
Do you mind if I call you Annabelle?

THREE HOURS AFTER THE FUNERAL OF AUNT JANE I TRY TO SWING LIKE SONNY ROLLINS

Rain of frown and fumbled word
strums forget-me-not tunes
on the kitchen screens,
taps on this old back door
to find my aunt Jane gone
and me lost in memories.

Wind of black dog and deacon
cuffs around the cottonwood
and scatters the elm leaves,
then the long day yellows
to grow stovepipe hot,
and stillness tramps the floor.

When my wife of damp and droop
returns from sultry's town
with a box of soapflakes
and three cans of sardines,
I stay in the cool cellar
to play my first saxophone.

ELDON'S CIRCUS

Tornado wild
Eldon hotrods
out of Bean Blossom
on twisty roads
with a mad desire
to make the soft
and jumping ground
leap up on leaves
spin clouds toward sky

Eldon
Eldon
she said
Eldon
I do not love you anymore
Eldon
she said
Eldon
Eldon

And so Eldon
a clown who wears
his own red nose
and funny hair
brings unannounced
to Brown County
his speed circus
of flashing wheels
and flying dust

IN WINTER SLEEP

Oak leaves, pine cones, blown feathers, acorns, snowflakes
fall over the shallow graves of antelope.

From an iron-gray waste, Canada geese fly south
across the steep prairies of a hunter's moon.

WALKING ON THE GREAT PLAINS

At dawn I quit the house for short grass.
The water tower palms the pale moon.
Morning fries me a Nebraska sun-egg.
I pause and turn around slowly,
seeing too far in all directions,
feeling dwarfish against the blown sky.
Alliance, Hay Springs, Scottsbluff, Chadron:
wonderful buffalo nickel towns
coined in a dream of prairie schooners.
Dust rises in this rainmaker's world.
Heat is a lightning rod, vibrating.
The sunflower stares a hole in my skull.

THE RED NUDE

When I haven't any blue, I use red.
—Pablo Picasso

Red candles. Smoky red lights.

Sipping a glass of claret,
the nude girl moves to the window.

Sunset. Scarlet poppies. Bloodroot.

Pomegranates along a brick wall:
the flushed faces of old gardeners.

Under the cold strawberry stars,
crimson eyes of dying animals.

A dream of cardinals and cherries.

The ruby moon slips between
bare thighs of garnet and rosewood.

Red candles. Smoky red lights.

from
**STRAWBERRIES (1970)
VOYAGES TO THE INLAND SEA (1971)
CRABTREE'S WOMAN (1972)
WELL YOU NEEDN'T (1975)
BRIGHT MISSISSIPPI (1975)**

Men are not flattered by being shown that there has been a difference of purpose between the Almighty and them.

—Abraham Lincoln

CHICKEN

The carhop floated up
like a white, plump, summer cloud.
"Honey," I said, "I've been out east
and I'm hung over.
I've been to Vermont and New Hampshire
and even to the coast of Maine.
They're crusty places, all of them,
and not easily impressed with strangers
who come blowing in from spots
like, say, Mankato and Moose Jaw.
And I've been in and out
of more damn green-shuttered windows."
Honey was patient,
just recently escaped from pig farms
and familiar with shitstorms.
She shifted a healthy cud
of some of Mr. Wrigley's finest
and pushed her boobies against the VW.
"You a second-story man?"
she said, trying to act sexy.
"No," I said, "I'm a true-story man,
honest and reliable as your daddy's watch."
"Well you talk a good game,
that's for sure," she said.
"Put your best wings in a big box,"
I said, suddenly very hungry.
"You mean chicken?" she said.
"It's that kind of place," I said.
I stretched my stiff limbs
and flexed my biceps.
"Hey, you're a large one," she said.
"A chief is no bigger than his blanket,"
I said, waving her away.

JUNKMAN'S SPRING

Thick blades
of coarse grass
knife up
between
cracked bricks
in the alley
where the junkman
gently prods
his half-blind horse
through a soft
April noon
intense
with plump buds
that are popping
their heads off
under a popgun sun
and the old
worn out junkman
stirs once more
with a new heat
in what has been
a cold spring
but which
comes on now
with a bright
and conquering
jazz beat
and what good
green drummer
do you hear
Mr. Frog?

TWO DAYS OUT OF THREE CHURCHES

The Illinois
state trooper,
a fresh chaw
of Mail Pouch
swelling
his grizzled jaw,
investigates
the abandoned
pickup truck
which,
as it turns out,
is not abandoned
at all,
but two days out
of Three Churches,
West Virginia,
trouble
is just bound
to come,
especially
when you elope
at sixteen
and your
green-eyed
big-dimpled
baby doll
starts to cry
and cry
and you
have to stop
and make her
feel good
all over
again,
again.

IOWA SATURDAY NIGHT

The teenage girls
of Grundy Center,
breast deep in bubbles,
are rubbing boys
into their skin.

Over stockpiles of hair curlers
and twisted toothpaste tubes,
slender fingers write
I love you
on steamed-up mirrors.

In frilly bedrooms,
please observe
yellow dresses and pink panties:
butterflies
on a summer lawn.

PHONE BOOK BLUES

I'm in a smoke-blue town.
Out of money.
Out of gas.
And I'm looking at the phone book,
flipping the phone book pages to
Snyder, Albert
Snyder, Bruce K.
Snyder, Daphne
Snyder, Stephen C
Snyder, Wilma
and your name is not among the Snyder people.
Are you here?
Are you mad?
Are you jailed?
Are you sad?
Or are you picking the cabbage
down in Deaf Smith County?
Well, I'm dead in a smoke-blue town.
Yes, I'm a goner now.
Where's the river?
Where's the lake?
Oh where's the water, Wilma Snyder?

ONE DOZEN VALENTINES

A diamond of ice on our mailbox.
A rainbow bubble between your breasts.
A paper candle pinned to a child's coat.
A marble lodged in the ear of a tree.
A taffy apple on the seat of an old Ford.
A crayon picture of Bess Truman.
A flower of jam on the judge's corncob pipe.
A beer sign in a lost mining town.
A full moon rising over the turkey sheds.
A dandelion pressed in a telephone book.
A scarlet kiss-print above my thigh.
A signed copy of this poem.

SEEN ABOARD THE *TEXAS CHIEF* DURING AN UNSCHEDULED STOP

A man not walking so good
comes out of the auto body shop
carrying a carton of buttermilk,
glances up at the dark, blowing sky
as if expecting a special cloud
to drift by with his name on it,
a name like Harvey B. Thanet, I'll bet,
then fumbles the key into the door lock
of a mud-spattered Chevy pickup,
gets the door open at last,
wraps up the buttermilk
in a pair of paint-stained overalls
and puts it on the front seat,
slams the door and locks it,
looks up at the storm-brewing sky,
picks his pockets for a cigar
or maybe a stick of Black Jack gum,
finds neither one and shrugs,
walks again through the shop entrance
like a wounded Illinois mallard,
and so is gone forever from my sight,
but not, for some reason, from my mind,
and if you don't want a Mr. Thanet
to come limping into your dull life,
don't ride around in Santa Fe Pullmans,
or at least be on guard enough
so you can whip the shade down.

ASK ME NOW

I poked squirming leaves in my ears,
sucked dry the nectar of sweet blossoms,
curled up in the big bosoms of trees.

I wanted spring to make me gasp for breath,
to make me ache in root and branch,
to cut me up with long knives of sun.

But it was her diamond ring that did it,
that shattered my eyes, broke my nose,
and her laughter left me weak and dying.

WELL YOU NEEDN'T

I'll play it and tell you what it is later.
                —Miles Davis

Find Uncle Fred's photograph
in the tan attic trunk.

What kind of town is Ashtabula?

Dust Uncle Fred's photograph
with a clean green Kleenex.

What kind of name is Ashtabula?

Put Uncle Fred's photograph
next the aspidistra.

What kind of fun is Ashtabula?

RUBY, MY DEAR

Oh, sing of Falstaff,
Bud, and Schlitz.
Red boy waves at the train,
boy in blue waves,
and green pants boy waves,
waves at the *Land O'Corn.*
Star beer: "Equals the best
and is better than the rest."
Now girl waves, pink girl
waves and flowing blonde
hair waves like wheat,
prairie grass, corn silk,
waves among train boys.
Oh, sing of Grain Belt,
Hamm's, and Blatz.
Hey, what's my daughter
doing in Dubuque,
waving, waving waves?

I MEAN YOU

I mean you
in New Boston
and Cairo.
I mean you
in Beardstown
and Quincy.
I mean you,
I mean the river,
I mean towboats,
I mean willows
at Hannibal
and Clinton.
I mean you
and sunsets
in Muscatine
and Sabula.
I mean you,
I mean laughing,
I mean boozing,
I mean fighting
in Keokuk
and Port Byron.
I mean you
and I mean me.
Me and you,
kissing it up
in La Crosse
or Nauvoo.

JACKIE-ING

The moon sails through the fog
and I can see clearly now
that the wild green apples
in the wind-torn orchard
are the vagabond eyes
of Alice who went away
to rage in snorting barns
with tall horses of the sun
hating me
forgetting Bill of the Elms
and Giles and Ford
those glum railroad strangers
who play hearts all night long
in the cold kitchen corner
with good Peggy from Pike
who says my name twice
like she means old pal
Jack Jack

IN WALKED BUD

Dan takes his big bongos down,
down to the goodbye river,
so he can sit in with Mr. Catfish,
so he can jam with Mr. Coolfish.

A crumble of pink bricks,
big patches of ugly weeds,
and these sick yellow flowers.
Say, what kind of sidewalk is this?

Bud, is that Bonnie's new cornhusk doll
with her funny head gone mush,
with her belly gone mush,
with her cute fanny gone mush?

Oh, farewell to the cemetery moon,
to the forgotten milk trains.
Oh, farewell, farewell, farewell
to the doomed lovers of Dunn Street.

SLOW TRAIN TO PITTSBURGH

The gents in the day coach who got on at Fort Wayne
were talking weather, crops, and politics.
"We haven't had a president since Truman," one says.
"Amen, brother," says another.
"Make that Abe Lincoln," a third says.
Little children with dirty faces
waved at the train in Lima, Ohio,
a town where the courthouse had lost its clocks.
Across the aisle was an abandoned newspaper.
I checked the baseball news carefully.
The Pirates had lost again, this time in ten innings.
"Damn," I said. "Damn, damn, damn."
"What's that, buddy?" says the guy with the ear trumpet.
"Pittsburgh's under water," I said.
"We're going to have to transfer to a yacht."
"Bought?" he says. "Bought what?"
I grabbed my electric razor and left the car.
Upon returning from a shave in the men's washroom,
I overheard something about a dirt clod fight:
somebody hurt, angry words, threats, and all that.
"When and where did all this take place?" I said.
"Coal City, about thirty-eight years ago,"
says this redneck farmer type,
pulling the cellophane off a Roi Tan.
I slipped *For Whom the Bell Tolls*
out of my new Zero King corduroy jacket,
read two more paragraphs in chapter two,
then decided I would have to have a drink.
We passed many freight cars while I was in the club car:
Erie-Lackawanna: "The Friendly Service Route,"
Gulf Mobile and Ohio,
Central of Georgia,
Monon: "The Hoosier Line,"
Delaware and Hudson,
Norfolk and Western.
The bar attendant hated all buses, all airplanes.
"A peasant's way of going about," he said,

poking a blue-striped towel inside a shot glass.
We shook on this and I ordered another Stroh's beer.
The train kept on stopping. I kept on drinking.
When I got off at Penn Central Station, my wife says,
"Why, Daddy, I do believe you are loaded."
"Yeah," I said, "like a carpenter's apron on a big job."
It was night in Pittsburgh.
I had crossed many rivers, many bridges to get there.
All the lights of the city were winking at me,
and I was sure I could hear soft music playing
out on the old Monongahela.
I walked around outside the station,
shouting at all the cab drivers,
"Pittsburgh! What's ever happened in Pittsburgh?"
A huge drop of Pennsylvania rain splashed my nose.
"It's late," my wife says. "It's a quarter to twelve.
Shall we go home now, Daddy?"
"No," I said, "I don't want to go home now.
I want to go straight back to Lima, Ohio,
where nobody knows what time it is."

THE PORCH

The boy with cerebral palsy
has a mop of sandy hair
and round, childlike eyes.

On these warm, bumblebee mornings
they push him out in a wheelchair
to a porch of potted plants.

Across North Seventh Street
the old lady has hung
Jesus Saves on every wall.

Behind her lace curtains
she reads her Bible out loud:
Genesis, Ruth, Lamentations.

And she repeats this from Luke 4:18,
" . . . to set at liberty
them that are bruised."

Now the screen door opens and slams,
and she's off again
to cure him with holy words.

The cannibal inside his skull
must be devouring a Congo
of overzealous missionaries.

They meet once every day.
He knows she's as unavoidable
as the next jerk of his head.

BRIGHT MISSISSIPPI

It's certainly a lead-pipe cinch, pardner,
that I'm in a dark blue funk.
I can no longer root hog or die
till the cows come home to this farm.
You got to know the ropes to go against the grain,
and scratchin' around in the soil
ain't exactly been my cup of Budweiser.
But I can still cut the mustard
and won't take no back seat
to some highfalutin, fly-by-night dude
who don't know if he's afoot or on horseback.
I'm turnin' over a brand-new leaf, you see.
I've got other fish to fry
when I get across that bright Mississippi water.
And I ain't singin' you no tune
the old cow died of, neither.
Remember, pardner, you done got the real goods,
straight from the horse's mouth,
which, while no manna from heaven,
is nevertheless within an ace of the gospel.

A FARM IN THE GREEN MOUNTAINS

Stone upon stone,
this weathered wall of stone
was built by men deviled by stone
from poor fields yielding mostly stone.

Stone upon stone,
this Vermont wall of stone
was the sure employment of stone
in a place that is shaped by stone.

Stone upon stone,
this ragged wall of stone
was a grudging tribute to stone
by farmers making peace with stone.

from
**CENTRAL STANDARD TIME (1978)
OPEN TO THE WIND (1978)
RIDING THE ROCK ISLAND THROUGH KANSAS (1979)
BOONDOCKS (1982)**

There is no easy way for us to make sense of our historic success in putting up with ourselves, our foolishness, our fraudulence, and finally our innocence.

—William Saroyan

RED BRICKS

A drizzly November day,
and a man has dead things
clogging up his dusty
warehouse brain.
With his nose flattened
against a pane
of cracked glass,
six floors off the street,
a man, a good man,
has gone mad
in an avalanche
of suicide bricks.
Yes, in damp-soul November
a river-eyed man,
a prairie-grass man,
gives up the ghost
in a rusty rain
in old red-brick Chicago.

POEM ON MY FATHER'S EIGHTIETH BIRTHDAY

The year turns summer again.
Today is your day of birth.
Who is Harold P. Etter?
Sons and daughters know.
A hot, steamy afternoon.
Palomino horse chews grass.
Last night a full moon.
We heard corn talking.
Our town breathes dark soil.
These rugged oak trees.
Father, I salute you now.
Your name grows tall here.

BARN DREAMS

Barns.
So many dreams of barns
blazing in the prairie sun.
Red barns, stone barns, round barns,
barns empty or falling down,
barns with cupolas,
hay-eating barns,
barns smelling of horses and old leather.
And winter barns, too,
crusted with ice and snow,
open to the wind.
Dreams, the dreams come on.
Me, all ages of me
entering barns,
sometimes in a daze of remembrance,
either corn or cattle outside,
a calico cat inside,
or perhaps the girl I lost
a long time ago
at the Illinois State Fair,
sitting quietly on a bale of straw,
her hair in pigtails,
her breasts rising like gold moons
above her soft and clinging dress,
saying, "I've missed you so very much."
May the green winds of chance
blow me always toward
barns.

LONG JOHN SILVER

"The wage scale here stinks," I said,
grabbing the attention of this old girl
decked out in new shoes and a percale dress.
"Oh, it's not so bad as that," she says,
and pops another gumdrop in her mouth.
"Long John Silver would wreck this joint," I said.
"He wouldn't put up with this nonsense.
Not for five minutes he wouldn't."
"Wrong John who?" she says, obviously puzzled.
"You don't know him at all," I said.
I was cranky because of the heat last night:
eyes bloodshot, back sore as hell
from sleeping in the bathtub to keep cool.
"Type this letter over, it's full of mistakes,"
the boss screams at Miss Percale Dress.
"It's a crime the way things are," I said.
"Better get your friend John," she says,
and flattens a marshmallow on her desk.

TUMBLEWEEDS

Tumbleweeds listen when the wind speaks.
Tumbleweeds love to roll around and get dirty.
Tumbleweeds have faces full of scratches.
Tumbleweeds carry no luggage, make no reservations.
Tumbleweeds are scared to death of fire.
Tumbleweeds dream of great tornadoes.
Tumbleweeds look like funny nets left on shore.
Tumbleweeds couldn't care less if they get lost.
Tumbleweeds don't go around looking for their roots.
Tumbleweeds often suffer from terrible dizzyness.
Tumbleweeds despise walls and fences.
Tumbleweeds know all about hello and goodbye.
Tumbleweeds never write home for money.
Tumbleweeds utter no regrets, make no promises.
Tumbleweeds say "Come chase me if you can."
Tumbleweeds feel they can always get away.

OLD KING COAL

I cross a black bridge
under black cloud, black sky.

City of the black tree.
City of the black house.
Black bells ring blackly
from the blackened church.

I sit on a black bench
and read a black book
on how to mine for coal.

A black bird drops a black turd
and flies away on a black oath.

"Bright sun never does shine
on this side of town,"
the old black man tells me.

Coal from the coal-black hole.
The chemistry of coal.
The pit of black dreams
breeds a slow black death.

Now I am coal, too, wrapped
in a shroud of black smoke.

GREEN-EYED BOY AFTER READING
WHITMAN AND SANDBURG

Beyond the empty crossroads store
and the stubble of new-cut weeds,
a man in a rough shirt and wide straw hat
whistles me to a long morning walk.

Clean smell of hay. This joyful flesh.
The sweet sound of the hermit thrush.
A virgin river sings in my free-verse head.

Deep in the honeysuckle shade
we fish for our lost American souls.

Yes, I'm sure there's a place for me
in this knockabout, haphazard world.

Oh, but look how the summer wind
bends the branches of the sycamore trees.

A black dog howls behind the barn.

A SUMMER TOURIST IN SORRENTO, MAINE

Morning mist hangs in the wooden ears of the church.

The bouy's bell rings like a tidal wave of Sundays,
and the harbor breeds a school of small white boats.

Birch trees have the worn faces of old lobstermen.

The lady with a seagull's eyes looks me over carefully,
saying nothing, waiting for me to say what I'm up to.

My jaws are jammed with blueberries.

STATEMENT

The roasted,
oat-toasted aroma
of this old Corn Belt
mill town,
which spreads
its commercial
oatmeal shanks
over both banks
of a brown river,
has sickened me
much too long,
as have blue memories
of the peanut man
who kept a small
tumbledown stall
by the railroad tracks
all summer long,
then one dark day
in early May
flung himself
under the wheels
of an eastbound freight,
so it's more than
just likely,
or even fate,
that come next fall
I'll leave this town
like Danny did,
and Phil and Sid,
and maybe not
come back at all.

BOONDOCKS

Now if you live in the country
and the farmer next door plants soybeans
right up to your back porch,
well, then you learn to like soybeans.
But this year he plants corn,
and since you've always liked corn,
you break out in little snatches of song
as you pad about your 1912 frame house,
which creaks like an old ship in the wind.
"What's to be so happy about?"
says the wife, suspicious, looking around
for something new she's missed.
"Oh, it's nothing at all," you say.
So she frowns and dusts another table,
and you head for that first ice-cold beer
which tastes so good about 9:00 a.m.
"It's not like you to sing," she says.
"Boondocks," you say. "Boondocks."

THE ELLSWORTH BROTHERS

The winter night they ran out of firewood,
Oscar threw in his orange-crate table,
Clarence chucked in a wooden lamp,
and Bert chopped up some old bed slats,
Ah, the coziness of a cheery fireplace,
good talk, good smokes, and lots of strong beer.
But it wasn't too long till the fire burned out
and the room turned colder and colder.
"How about Mama's rocking chair?" Sam said,
and he went for the ax by the door.
Oscar looked at Clarence, Clarence looked at Bert.
Without a word, they scooped Sam up
and locked him in the cellar with the apples,
the potatoes, and the jars of home brew.
"Now then, where were we?" Oscar said,
his eyes glued to a heavy picture frame.

THAT OLD-TIME FEELING

"I'm going to grab one of those
old, abandoned railroad coaches
and park it under the oak tree
that shades my big backyard," I said.

"Sure, so you can have a retreat
to write those good down-home poems,
poems on dirt farmers, coal smoke,
and the courthouse spittoon," she said.

"Poems? What poems? I'm going
to sit back in a green plush seat,
tell the conductor to wake me
when we're to Wichita," I said.

HOME COOKING

"You'll like her cooking, my friend," he says,
"providing you can stomach or put up with
greasy, burned, or just plain lumpy."

What are friends for if not for friends?

"Joella, come down, come down at once.
Joella, we have us a houseguest.
Joella, this is Mr. Etter from Illinois."

The long and loud percussion of pots and pans.

Nightfall with no country moon, no stars.
Want to zip back to Yankee pot-roast Kane County.
I feel greasy, burned, and lumpy.

I skip dessert, insist I'm on a diet.

Mr. Etter leaning against a green snow-fence.
Mr. Etter bending over a clump of weeds.
Mr. Etter sick as a dog in Tennessee.

TWENTY LINES FOR THOMAS HART BENTON

Jimmy Joe hoed
the stubborn weeds
in the corn rows
all sultry morning
until
the weather changed
from sun to rain
and lightning struck
a dead elm tree,
then he raced
toward the farmhouse,
knees pumping,
hoe in hand,
soaked to the skin,
only slowing up
to slap
the blind mule
on his broad rump
for luck
and no more weeds.

THE LAST SHOW IN TIJUANA

She shimmys and rolls her hips to
a drum-heavy beat: gyrations
of artless sex. We've come to leer.

We stare at her thick breasts, shiny
copper belly, jelly breasts, and
drink bottles of Tecate beer.

This stripper, a girl not sixteen,
shakes her plump can in our faces.
We smile weakly, too drunk to cheer.

THE SEVENTH RACE AT LINCOLN, NEBRASKA

The *Daily Racing Form* is more rag than newspaper now. I've studied the thing so hard my eyeballs ache. A lot of good it's done me. Haven't won a race all day. Time to get serious. Make a truly intelligent bet. They just played "Call to the Post." Must get a good look at the ponies this time. Seven horses go in the Seventh. One mile. Three year olds bred in Nebraska. A $9,000 purse. The Program selector picks them to finish: *Prom Crasher, Jackie B. Gaughan,* and *Marine Tested.* What does he know? Let's see, my favorite number is seven. *Marine Tested* is seven. Keep that in mind. My favorite color is red. That's *Cowgirl Cascio.* Good looking horse. Now for names. Best name here is *Jackie B. Gaughan.* Rolls right off the tongue. Sounds like the moniker of a girl banjo player out of Big Chimney, West Virginia. Hey, number five looks exceptionally eager to run. Lots of squirming and head bobbing. The trainer's got a great trainer's name. How can you top a handle like Dwight Clum? I'll bet no one has to tell him the difference between a fetlock and a saddle sore. The horse's name doesn't measure up, though. I'll not bet money on some hay-burner called *Alien Comet.* Decisions. Decisions. All this heavy brainwork makes me thirsty. I buy a large Falstaff beer and return to my seat. The character across the aisle, in the cowpuncher's hat and rose-pink shirt, brings back a plate full of baked beans, potato salad, and half a chicken with a slab of rye bread on top. He's come to the track to eat, not bet. The skinny bird next to him is no handicapper either. He picks his nose, not the ponies. I like the odds on horse number two. That's *Petty Theft.* You can make some pretty fair loot at 10 to 1. Why not bet the nag to show? Perhaps to place? Forget it. Again, I don't cotton to the name. Why are names so important to me? I must get rid of this totally unprofessional hang-up. *Prom Crasher* is number three. Blue silks. The jockey, R. D. Williams, is second in the jockey standings. Right behind Freddy Turner, who is sitting this race out. Nope. Blue isn't lucky for me. Also, I don't bet the jockey. Lost six straight times on Eddie Arcaro one time at Santa Anita. Let's check some past performances in the *Daily Racing Form.* No, let's not mess with that again. I'm confused. As usual. Time is running short. Got to get a bet down. The gent in front of me whispers some "inside dope" to his lady friend. This boy is not about to hand out any free information. So what. He's just playing Mr. Big Shot. I know his type. What about *Vision of Hope?* How about *Cowgirl Cascio?* I guess not. I'm in love with *Jackie B. Gaughan.* Only carries 109 pounds. That could be important. I glance up at the tote board to check the odds: 3 to 1, now 4 to 1, now back to 3 to 1. Wouldn't pay much. Two minutes left. Why not just go with lucky number seven? Right. Seven in the Seventh. Be smart. Get a hunch and bet a bunch, as the saying goes. Wish I had the guts to risk fifty bucks. Wish I had fifty bucks. Or even ten, for that matter. I run up the stairs. Almost knock over an old lady in jogging shoes, purple sunglasses, and a bowling shirt that says "Flo" on the front. Where on earth do these people come from? She's from Omaha, most likely. Or Sarpy County. Yep, I've decided on *Marine Tested.* No. I'll stick with *Jackie B. Gaughan.* At the two-dollar window, I clear my throat and say, "Number four to win." That's it. It's done. I got my dough on *Vision of Hope.* All the horses are set in the starting gate. The bell rings. They're off. I take a deep breath. Drain the rest of my beer. Where the devil is number four? Wish I had some field glasses. Here they come. The final straightaway. *Vision of Hope* is not going to make it. Not even close. Another slap in the face with a wet fish. No, I don't care who won. I tear my ticket twice. Drop the pieces under my seat. The Nebraska sun pours through the clubhouse windows. Over to the left, a young couple, in matching powder-blue pants and western-style belts, embraces. They jump up and down. They shout, "We won! We won!" I try my best to ignore them. Back to the *Daily Racing Form.* In the Eighth race, *Rain Circle* looks pretty good. Currently 7 to 2. Has had a couple of snappy outings of late. Maybe.

Maybe not. Then there's number three. Carries 119 pounds. Three less than *Rain Circle.* Should go at 2 to 1. Both these horses will end up as the favorites. No doubt about that. Hate to bet favorites. But I really need a winner. Badly. Look, I'm not going to fool around anymore. Number three it is. Hey, hold on a second. Stop the music right there. Do I really want to wager two bucks on a thoroughbred called *Miss Laurie Bale?* If I was full smart instead of just half smart, I'd skip this race and concentrate on picking the Exacta in the Ninth. Yes, of course. That's the way to go. But, first, I'll grab myself another beer. I think much better with my mitt around a cold Falstaff.

Fairgrounds, 17th Day, Friday, August 11, 1978

from

HOME STATE (1985)

By lust alone we keep the mind alive,
And grieve into the certainty of love.
—Theodore Roethke

Men are not lonely, but thinking is lonely.
—Gottfried Benn

It is a mighty poor man who ain't going to talk about
girls now and then.
—A Shoeshine Man

My whole life has hung too long upon a partial victory.
—William Carlos Williams

I will complain, yet praise,
I will bewail, approve;
And all my sowre-sweet dayes
I will lament, and love.
—George Herbert

COURTHOUSE CLOCKS

Like Harvey, the invisible rabbit who goes everywhere with Mr. Elwood P. Dowd, Doreen goes wherever I go. That I haven't actually seen her in the flesh for almost forty years —since the eighth grade, to be exact—makes no difference at all.

Tonight, coming out of the Paradise theater, after taking in a double-feature plus Bugs Bunny cartoon, with lots of popcorn, strawberry soda pop, and Milk Duds, we walk down Prairie Street to the town square, kicking and crunching the fallen maple leaves. Through the blue-gray fog that drifts up from the river, we can see the lit-up courthouse clocks. They look like eerie jack-o'-lanterns at a giant's castle or the huge yellow headlights of nineteenth-century passenger trains. "I hate courthouse clocks," Doreen says. "They're so pontifical. All those round, fat faces telling me how fast my life is racing by. And those solemn *bong, bong, bongs* every hour give me the creeps." I draw her closer to me, give her a little bite on the ear. "Let's remember to always love one another as hard as we can," I say. "You got it, my man, you got it," she says, and she backs me against a lamppost and really kisses me a good one.

That Doreen, she beats everything. She always does more than I expect her to do. And I really need her tonight. This living alone—with a Smith-Corona 2200 electric typewriter— is no fun, I tell you.

SCARECROW

There's my man over there. Yes, Mr. George Q. Scarecrow, the patient, wide-eyed, lovable retainer of these Corn Belt cornfields. Hey, look, old pal, Doreen wants to plant a big bubble-gum kiss on your silly mouth, and I would love to borrow your hobo's hat to wear to the Firemen's Ball. Say, by the way, Mr. Scarecrow, do you really scare away many crows from all this corn? Do you ever want to go on strike for better wages, a shorter work week, a beefed-up medical insurance plan? And do you now and then get so restless that you want to run away from the whole thing and then find out you can't? Someday when you're not so busy, my friend, we're going to have us a long talk. I just have to know what it's like to be a scarecrow.

HAMBLETONIAN

"Where you from?" I asked the man next to me, a tall stranger with a short beard who was holding down a stool at the Sunflower Cafe. "Du Quoin," he said. "Where they run the famous Hambletonian championship trotting races every year." "Where they *used* to run them," I said, taking a big bite out of my prune Danish. "Yeah," he said, "where they used to. They got it back east now. New York, New Jersey, someplace like that." "I hear Du Quoin's a fairly decent town," I said. "It's all right," the man said, stabbing a half-smoked Old Gold into the yellow remains of a fried egg. "Well," I said, "I've been meaning to see the Hambletonian for years. Now, I guess it's too late." "Yeah, it's too late," he said. "You gotta go back east you wanna see it." "It's a crime," I said. "Yeah, it's a crime, all right," he said. "It's one hell of a goddamn crime," I said, stirring some lump sugar into my coffee.

TALLGRASS PRAIRIE PLOT

"I'm going to start a tallgrass prairie plot," I said to Doreen before hitting the hay on a warm and windless night in mid-May. "I'm going to plant big bluestem, little bluestem, Indian grass, prairie coneflower, purple coneflower, sloughgrass, false sunflower, downy sunflower, compass-plant, rattlesnake-master, and prairie dock." "Sounds like a good idea, but who's going to do all the work, and especially who's going to do all the weeding?" she said, pulling the spread off the bed. "I'll be doing half of it," I said. "Half of it?" she said. "I'll need some help, of course, and that's where you come in," I said. "Oh no you don't," she said. "You're not going to get me out there to sweat on my hands and knees like a Roman slave while you sit around inside smoking your pipe, sipping herb tea, and banging on the typewriter." "Well, I guess there's no real big hurry to start a tallgrass prairie plot," I said. "I may put it off for a year or two." "You mean forever, don't you?" she said. "Who knows?" I said. "I know," she said, and she slipped down the zipper on her tall grass-stained blue jeans.

STATE FAIR

It's a come-one, come-all party, is what it is, or a gigantic family picnic with expensive out-of-town entertainment. The state fair in Springfield is also an annual meeting of the clans, where the state's people and the state's farm animals gather to look each other over. Grandmas look at pigs. Cows look at uncles. Sisters look at horses. Goats look at fathers. When the good citizens of Jo Daviess County and McLean County and Gallatin County get tired of gazing at the finest products of our Illinois barnyards and pastures, they head toward corn dogs, lemonade, peanuts, cotton candy, popcorn, cheeseburgers, pizza, caramel apples, and Eskimo Pies. The children jump up and down and say that state fair balloons are fun to hold and look at, but what they really want is to ride on the Sky Diver, the Scrambler, the Rock-o-Plane, the Twister, the Ferris wheel, the Spider, and especially the Tilt-a-Whirl. Doreen says she's hungry and to hell with rides and exhibits and what's going on where a rock band is getting themselves all steamed up. She informs me she'll settle for a T-bone steak smothered in onions and a large order of home fries on the side plus a chocolate sundae with mashed hickory nuts and a cute little cherry on top of the whipped cream. "You're always thinking of that tummy of yours," I tell her. "Let's go over and shake hands with the governor, instead." I say this as a joke, but Doreen says, "Well, okay, why not." We stand in line, and at last get to meet the big man face to face. "Nice to meet you," I say, trying to act sincere, though my heart's not in it. "I'm starving to death," Doreen says. "Not so loud," the governor says, forcing a forced political smile.

MAX

Every dog, both male and female, in this neighborhood is named Max. There are no dogs named Spot or Rover or Prince or Lobo, and certainly, thank the good Lord, none named Fido. Nobody says nothing to nobody about how come every dog around here answers to the name Max. It's the way things are, that's all. If you have a dog, you name the dog Max. It's just that simple. Since every dog is named Max, the dogs know they have no special names. Max means dog and dog means Max. Yet, each Max knows when he or she is being called, and the other Max dogs pay no attention and go about their business. Yesterday, a new family moved in across the street. Today, they bought themselves a dog. His name is Max. We all made sure of that.

A BEARDSTOWN DREAM

It was my friend Richard Bissell who put me onto Beardstown. "It's up the Illinois River and most of the people are catfish," says Bill Joyce, deckhand and chief character in Bissell's *A Stretch on the River*. Well, of course, I had to take a look for myself, and sure enough the man was right. I watched some mighty fine catfish types come out of their catfish houses and walk along East Catfish Street. I saw them eating catfish burgers and sipping catfish colas at the Catfish Drive-In. I saw them wearing catfish shirts and pants and catfish hats and coats. Some of the men and boys sported catfish boots and belt buckles. The women carried catfish handbags, and most of the young girls wore long catfish earrings. Since it was May Day, I went out to the Curtis Catfish grade school and watched the carefree students dance around a catfish maypole. Later, after I checked out of the Catfish Motor Court, I pulled into the Catfish Amoco filling station and was told I needed two quarts of catfish oil. "I don't believe this Beardstown," I said to the gas-pump jockey with the blue catfish tattoo on his arm. "Believe it," he said, and handed me my change: three crisp catfish dollars and two shiny catfish dimes.

CHICAGO

City of the bent shoulders, the bum ticker, the bad back. City of the called third strike, the blocked punt. City of the ever-deferred dream. City of the shattered windshield, the loose wheel, the empty gas tank. City of I remember when, of once upon a time. City of not "I will," but "I wish I could."

*

In the Chicago spring of 1949, I worked nights loading trucks at a department-store warehouse on Harrison Street. It was after midnight when I caught an elevated train and headed north to my nine-dollar-per-week roominghouse on Grace Street, and two in the morning before I fell asleep in a room so small it could have been used for a closet—the bath was about half a mile down the hall. By the time I got up, it was almost time to go to work again. I hated this poor-boy life, and it was only made bearable by this little sixteen-year-old brunette who lived close by on Cornelia Avenue, near Halsted. I thought I was madly in love with her, and maybe I was for awhile. When we finally broke up, a week after we agreed to become engaged, there was nothing to keep me in Chicago. I quickly said goodbye to the warehouse on Harrison Street and the roominghouse on Grace and got the hell out to the cornfields, where I spent most of the summer walking around in my bare feet, saying to myself, "That was a close call, pardner. That was a very close call. Nineteen is too young to even think of getting married."

*

Chicago, build yourself a building even half as handsome and dignified as the Wrigley building and I will hop aboard the next train and go see it. But don't expect me to get excited about a monstrosity such as the Hancock building, let alone the Equitable building and the rest of those boring skyscrapers that keep shooting up like tall weeds in some crazy farmer's onion patch.

A quarter of a century ago, two drunks got off the bus in the Loop. "Which way to the Middle Border?" they asked a cabbie, half asleep in his *Chicago Tribune*, working on a three-day beard. One of those drunks was me. The other drunk was last seen somewhere out in scenic North Dakota, asking the same question to every Indian he could find.

*

There are no more Carl Sandburgs, Sherwood Andersons, Theodore Dreisers, George Ades, or Ben Hechts in residence anymore, but the hustlers still come to the big city by the big lake. They come with their neon shirts, their glass pants, their plastic eyes. Yes, and they come with their loaded dice, their two-headed coins, their marked cards. And the rigged games go on twenty-four hours a day, with no letup on Sunday, no time out for Thanksgiving or Christmas. "Business," they tell you. "Business is America and America is business. You got that straight, buddy?"

*

In Old Town, at a booze joint with an old-fashioned bubbling jukebox, the old argument flares up once again as to which side of town is best: North Side, South Side, or West Side? When my turn comes to cast my vote, I say "East Side." There's a few seconds of silence. "East Side?" says the guy with the Cubs cap on backwards. "East Side? Shit, there's no goddamn East Side. East Side is the fuckin' lake." I put down my Old Style beer. "That's right," I say. "East Side is the best side."

*

The Pullman car, the cafeteria, and group insurance are all gifts from Chicago to the nation. Having enjoyed all three for some time now, all I can say is, "That's fine and dandy, but what has Chicago done for us lately?"

"What can we do to please a hard case like you?" Old Mother Chicago says to me, shooing the pigeons off the mayor's limousine. "Well," I say, "for starters you can bring back the Blue Note and Jazz Limited and make the city a great jazz city again. You can also put up a statue to Harriet Monroe, the kind and courageous lady who founded *Poetry* magazine in 1912."

*

Look, friends, the big whoopee party that was once Chicago is over. I know there are a handful of diehards still hanging around, hoping for a scantily-clad girl to pop out of a fancy cake or for another case of imported champagne to show up, but let's get serious, let's be realistic, let's get our hats and coats and make for the door. Mr. Royko and Mr. Kupcinet (in butler's uniforms) will turn off the lights.

*

Yet if it's a choice between Chicago and battered and bummed-out New York, I'll take Chicago every time. And half-assed cities like Los Angeles and San Francisco and Miami and Houston aren't even in the running.

*

But there is still a glimmer of hope for Chicago. In 1983 the city elected its first black mayor, Harold Washington, and he may prove to be the best man to run City Hall since Kate O'Leary's cow was suspected of arson.

*

Well, if you must have the real dope, Doreen, it was so damn cold in there, I don't remember what I did.

BASEBALL

We stand for "The Star-Spangled Banner." The home-plate umpire shouts "Play Ball!" The leadoff batter spits tobacco juice through his teeth. The pitcher spits. The catcher spits. The first baseman spits into his glove and rubs it in with the heel of his hand. The second baseman spits on the infield dirt, and so does the rookie shortstop, who, being a bit nervous, just called up from the Iowa farm club, dribbles some spit on his chin. The third baseman spits. The pitcher spits again and checks the outfielders, who all spit at the same time. The first pitch of the game is a fastball strike, right over the outside corner of the plate. The batter turns his head, says a few angry words to the home-plate umpire, and spits. "Have an eye, ump," shouts the visiting team's manager from the dugout, and he spits a brown stream of Beech-Nut halfway to the third-base foul line.

DANDELIONS

My neater than neat neighbor, whose lawn always looks like the green cloth of a pool table, has crossed the street to give me some advice on how to rid my own lawn of dandelions. "You got more dandelions in your front yard than anyone in town," he says. "I like dandelions," I say. "What the hell for?" he says. "Well, they're beautiful, for one thing," I say. "They're weeds, not good for anything," he says. "I like weeds," I say. "I can't stand to look at your yard the way it is," he says. "Try to get through spring and summer and into fall and you can look at lots of leaves laying around, then," I say. He wrinkles his forehead, squints his eyes. "It's no wonder I've never seen a nut like you at any of our Rotary Club meetings or down at the American Legion," he says. "No wonder," I say. Damn these dumb neighborhood meddlers. Why don't they mind their own damn business? I make a mental note to exclude this dolt from my forthcoming Memorial Day cookout and potato-sack race. The poor sap would probably trip over a dandelion, anyway.

Now if you folks who have been straining your ears to listen in on this classic debate will excuse me, I think I'll go inside and have a tall glass of dandelion wine. I know Doreen is no doubt on her second glass by now, starting to get twitchy, taking the pins out of her dark hair, about ready to ask me, "You want to go upstairs for awhile, Mr. Dandelion?"

POPULISM

It's not that I'm unhappy being a Democrat, it's that I would be a whole lot happier being a Populist—a real bumping, jumping, thumping Populist, with lots of local meetings to attend in smoke-filled rooms and a national convention to go to every four years. The Populists had themselves some good old times back in the 1890s. They told the citizenry what was going wrong in the country and what had to be done before it was too late. They also shook up the smug gang of robber barons who believed that America was theirs to run as they saw fit, namely, to make sure that the money always ended up on their side of the table. After William Jennings Bryan (born in Salem, Illinois) was defeated for the presidency in 1896, most Populists became Democrats. I can understand that, but now it's time to bring back the Populist party again, the party of grass-roots democracy. There is much that needs changing, or, better, restoring. The first thing I would like to see restored is our once excellent rail transportation network, and I mean streetcars and interurbans as well as passenger trains. It is quite obvious that the demise of this nation's rail system was a plot initiated by the oil companies and Detroit automakers who bought the votes of public officials from coast to coast. Another thing I would like to see restored is a healthy farm population. The farmers have for too long been victimized by an ugly, uninformed, urban mentality that has permitted far too many of our rural citizens to fall into a permanently poor economic class. Yes, I want to bring back the Populist party, the Populist spirit, the Populist sense of fair play, and I hope I'm called a kook, a dreamer, a socialist, a troublemaker, a reactionary, a crank, an anarchist, a maniac, and much worse, because then I'll know for sure I'm thinking and acting correctly. Do I ramble too much? Do I get myself too worked up? Do I think I have some of the answers that would provide a better life for *all* the people? You folks out there never ran into a piss and vinegar Populist, have you?

HOTEL NAUVOO

Believe me when I tell you I'd like to write something cute and clever about the Hotel Nauvoo. But I can't. It's not that I don't know anything about the place, because I do. I know quite a bit about the Hotel Nauvoo. I've sipped their great whiskey sours in the cozy cocktail lounge, eaten their family-style chicken dinners in the spacious dining room, and slept in their comfortable beds upstairs, a cool Mississippi River breeze billowing the curtains, while outside the old Mormon ghosts tiptoed around under the gnarled and venerable trees. But that's all I'm going to tell you. Certain things have happened to me at the Hotel Nauvoo which I don't want to talk about. I'm sorry. I don't like to clam-up like this. But I'm afraid that's the way it's going to be. I know that all you travelers out there in highwayland aren't going to be too informative about some of the experiences you've had while spending the night at the Pere Marquette Lodge in Grafton, the Red Rooster Inn in Hillsboro, or the Gas Light Motel in Taylorville. Now that we have that settled, pass me that basket of hot biscuits. I better eat up and get back on the road.

MAIL

I've grown weary all these years of hearing that tired baloney about how slow the mail is in this country of ours. Gimme a break. It has always come plenty fast enough for me. In fact, it can creep in here a whole lot slower, for all I care. I could have waited another week, another month, or even forever for the hot news I got today, which included the following: letter saying Uncle Geoffrey is suffering from asthma, gout, and patchy baldness; postcard saying *The Paris Review* can't find the poems I sent nine months ago; letter saying the Shell Oil Company has canceled my credit card; postcard saying the Illinois Arts Council isn't going to give me money this year; letter saying my six cats will be shot, poisoned, or ground up into pussy burgers if I don't keep them in my own yard; postcard saying the essay I wrote on the modern Hawaiian novel needs more revision and research; letter saying my subscription to *Down Beat* has expired; postcard saying if I have written anything taking place in outer space, a New York literary agency will be pleased as punch to read it; letter saying how I can make big money in the mink-ranch business. So tell me why I needed to know all this stuff in such a screaming hurry? The mail is slow, is it? Don't make me laugh. Hey, United States Postal Service, you're doing just fine. Keep all those cards and letters coming—as slow as possible. This old mail-hound is making no complaints.

FREIGHT TRAINS

The iron thunder of freight trains fills my bedroom at night, rattles the windows of this white frame house which sits near the mainline tracks. I often make love to freight-train jazz. This morning I ate a stack of freight-train hotcakes. This afternoon I drank a bottle of freight-train beer. Now I sit on my screened porch and watch the long early-evening freights go by. I don't count cars anymore, but I will often call out those famous American names, those marvelous, memory-haunted, musical names: Chicago and Eastern Illinois, Denver and Rio Grande, Missouri Pacific, Chesapeake and Ohio, Wabash, Union Pacific, Boston and Maine, Rock Island, Louisville and Nashville, Central Vermont, Soo Line, Cotton Belt, Nickel Plate, Southern Pacific, Milwaukee Road, Erie-Lackawanna, Burlington Northern, Lehigh Valley, Norfolk and Western, Central of Georgia, Kansas City Southern, Baltimore and Ohio, Texas and Pacific, Illinois Central, and, always, that prince among railroad monikers, the ever-loving Atchison, Topeka and Santa Fe. Some smoky-red dawn, maybe in frozen-pipe February, I may be on my deathbed, right by the window, and wish for nothing more than one more yellow Chicago and North Western caboose, one more Pennsylvania gondola, one more beat-up but beautiful Frisco boxcar. No, I'll never shake these freight-train rhythms from my freight-train soul.

SCREEN DOOR

What a weekend of comings and goings! What a workout for the old screen door! Open, shut. *Squeak, bang.* Open, shut. *Squeak, bang.* Shoes, sandals, slippers, boots, bare feet, and moccasins (bought in Taos, New Mexico) have scraped and padded into the house and out again for the past two days. Let's see, there was the plumber, the Culligan soft-water man, the electrician, several aunts and uncles from Rockford and Freeport, one niece and three nephews in Monkey Ward bathing suits, a neighbor giving away strawberries and cucumbers, the aluminum-siding man, the air-conditioning man, the gas man, a kid wanting to mow the lawn, a Mutual of Omaha insurance agent, two pale young women pushing a strange religion, an Avon lady asking an address, and a Girl Scout selling horse-show tickets. *Squeak, squeak, squeak. Bang, bang, bang.* It's a real wonder that the poor screen door hasn't fallen off its hinges. Then along about nine o'clock in the warm and wormy darkness of this Sunday night, I hear the screen door squeak open again. "Who is it?" I say, dropping the latest copy of the *Daily Racing Form*. "Super Woman," says the sexiest voice in the middle of the Middle West. And the screen door bangs shut for the last time.

THREE POETS

Sandburg

Carl Sandburg came to Chicago on big Swede feet. He walked all over the city and looked at the Art Institute, the stockyards, the ball parks, the zoo, the Chicago River, the Loop department stores, Lake Michigan, the public library, the Water Tower, the Halsted streetcar, the back alleys, the railroad stations, the Clark Street taverns, the steel mills, the plush hotels and restaurants, the slums, the factories, the Maxwell Street fish market, the subway, the Monadnock building, Lincoln Park, and all the people he could find—some with Swedish names. Yes, Carl Sandburg sized up everything and everybody with his shrewd reporter's eyes and then, having gotten it all down pat, moved on.

Lindsay

"Doreen, did you know that Vachel Lindsay once worked for Marshall Field's department store?" I said. "What's that again?" she said, putting down her nail file, snapping off the track meet on television. "I said that Vachel Lindsay, the poet, once had a job with Marshall Field and Company. Isn't that interesting?" I said. "No, it isn't," she said. "Honestly, sometimes you can be so terribly boring. I think you could use some fresh air."

Masters

The only woman in the Spoon River cemetery who refused to tell her story to Mr. Edgar Lee Masters is now at last ready to spill her guts: "My name is Ida Dunn, and I'd a done told this Chicago poet fellow my tale of hell on earth except I never cared for them big-city types much, and him saying not to worry, that he was a lawyer by profession and grew up in this part of the state. The man said he'd be back, but he ain't never been back, and it just goes to show a body that you can't never put no trust in any writer, let alone some damn fool who sneaks around in graveyards and bothers the dead."

JOHN KNOEPFLE

It's time to put aside thoughts of Sandburg, Lindsay, and Masters for awhile and think about the state's *living* poets, Auburn's John Knoepfle, for instance, a truly wonderful wordworker on the central Illinois prairie. He is a man whose works touch and retouch the human heart in many miraculous ways. I have read all his poems, all his books. I try to read everything he writes. If news reached me that John had scratched six words in the dirt in front of the Lincoln-Berry store at New Salem State Park or on the wall of an old brick warehouse in Rock Island or East Moline, I would have to drop whatever I was up to at the moment and hurry off to see what those six words were all about.

John, old friend, old comrade of the printed page, I salute you tonight, here in this quiet, dream-haunted Corn Belt village. May lucky stars watch over you for many more Illinois days and nights.

PIKE COUNTY

What I'm after is a whole week in Pittsfield, Illinois. You see, I would like more than anything to write half a dozen poems about the Pike County Courthouse, which, by the way, isn't your average run-of-the-mill county courthouse but *the* all-American county courthouse. I first saw it several years ago when I was rambling through Pike County, on my way to see some Mississippi water. It is a very tall, three-story building, with a magnificent spire which can be seen when you're out in the country putting the corn picker to bed. Made of Indiana limestone, it was, according to the Illinois state guidebook, constructed in 1894. When I caught my first glimpse of it that day, I knew I had to stop and take some snapshots. Everyone else stayed in the car, mumbling and grousing about the "peculiar interests of some people" and issuing bulletins about the urgent need to get something cold to drink, take a leak, and lie down a bit before diving into a submarine sandwich over in Hannibal, Missouri. I have not mentioned this great desire of mine to return to Pittsfield and Pike County to anyone. I'm already up to here with funny looks and sarcastic comments. You know, sometimes it's pure hell being a poet out here in the alfalfa districts.

FISHING

We were out in the middle of the lake in an outboard, our fishing poles over the water, our hooks baited with worms. Yes, fishing at last. A couple of published writers taking some time off on a quiet summer day. We lit up Dutch Masters cigars and got cold cans of Pabst Blue Ribbon out of the beer bag. Fishing. You bet. A writer's sport. But the fish wouldn't bite, wouldn't even nibble. We soon lost interest. The empty beer cans began to accumulate and roll around in the boat. Fresh cigars were stripped of their cellophane wrappers and smoked down to stubs. The talk turned from fish to other topics—magazine editors, critics, forgotten novelists—and then at last to the mystery of words: words like "erstwhile" and "equivocate," like "myriad" and "mellifluous." And the talk turned to obscure nouns and strange verbs, to ridiculous adjectives and comical adverbs. The poles were put back in the boat. We no longer tried to fish for fish. We were after words now. It was a good day. Yes, a mighty fine fishing day. Each of us had caught a mess of words. When we returned to shore and stepped out of the outboard, we had words pinned to our shirts, words stuck in our hats and shoes, and words, words, and more words crammed into our pockets. "There's no limit on how many words you can catch," I said. "No, there isn't," my friend said, setting a can of words on the pier.

SUNFLOWERS

Barefoot, wearing skin-tight jeans cut off high on her tan thighs, Doreen bursts between two wind-crazed sunflowers. She is breathing hard. Her round, firm breasts rise and fall under her yellow T-shirt which carries the words: *Maid for Wrestling.* "Is that for me?" she says. "Is what for you?" I say. "The telephone, dummy, the telephone. Is it for me?" she says. Her knees are grass-stained, her eyes are wide with excitement, her long hair looks like it has lost a match to Hurricane Camille. Man, I want to swat her a good one on her plump behind. But instead I say, "The dummy heard no telephone. Now go kiss a sunflower."

CORNFIELDS

> *Corn, the most American thing in America.*
> —Thomas Wolfe

> *I can think of nothing more exciting than just sitting in a cornfield on a windy fall day and listening to the dry rustle.*
> —Andrew Wyeth

> *Poets have not sung of the corn. They are busy singing of themselves.*
> —Sherwood Anderson

There are more unsolved mysteries in a single Illinois cornfield than in all the haunted houses of old New England. There are green and gold secrets hidden inside the cornhusks. The corn tassels and corn silk defy rational explanations. On hot, humid, sticky summer nights you can hear the corn talking over ancient corn legends, telling stories about sweet corn, dent corn, flint corn, flour corn, and even popcorn. There are puzzles to be untangled in each ear of Illinois corn. Strange enigmas and unfathomed riddles can be found in every row of ripening corn.

*

When I came upon her in the corn, I loved her to death—tassel to corn silk—and later, burst clean out of our husks, we lay there, exhausted in the sweet milk of cornfield loving.

*

Outside Bloomington, Illinois, we drive past a towering cornfield in the early-autumn twilight. "The corn looks like a crowd of people running away," Doreen says. I agree with her and stop the car to write that down in the corn-colored notebook I keep in the glove compartment of my corn-colored Camaro.

ADLAI STEVENSON

When Stevenson said, while running for president, "The Democratic Party is the people's party, not the labor party, not the farmers' party, not the employers' party—it is the party of no one because it is the party of everyone," I knew I could follow him anywhere. And when he said (speaking of President Eisenhower), "Golf is a fine release from the tensions of office, but we are a little tired of holding the bag," I knew I would have a good time along the way.

Adlai Stevenson is by far the greatest man Illinois has produced in the twentieth century. I will always be proud and thrilled to think he was once living among us here in the Prairie State. He was a man of so much wisdom, humor, and kindness. Men of his high standards seldom appear on the political scene. If you doubt this, look around for yourself, and be sure to take a long look at the jackass who currently occupies the governor's chair in Springfield. Like many other good citizens of Illinois, I am looking forward to the day when "Big Jim" Thompson is no longer making a shambles of the state I love. But you really can't be too surprised at the low caliber of our officeholders. I agree with Theodore Roethke's statement: "A considerable section of influential American public men are simply hillbillies who have learned to count." All right, enough of the negative. Let's get back to a brighter time. Let's get back to Stevenson. Here are some more of his thoughtful words, which certainly need to be read again and again:

> *The government must be the trustee for the little man, because no one else will be. The powerful can usually help themselves—and frequently do!*
>
> *Those who corrupt the public mind are just as evil as those who steal from the public purse.*
>
> *Nixon is the kind of politician who would cut down a redwood tree, then mount the stump for a speech on conservation.*

If the Republicans stop telling lies about us, we will stop telling the truth about them.

I don't know yet whether one can win an election with hard, distasteful truths, but this is the only way I want to win it.

Patriotism is not the fear of something; it is the love of something.

Communism is the corruption of a dream of justice.

Technology, while adding daily to our physical ease, throws daily another loop of fine wire around our souls.

I believe in the forgiveness of sin and the redemption of ignorance.

My definition of a free society is a society where it is safe to be unpopular.

We cannot afford to be penny-wise and people-foolish.

Everyone has something to contribute to the welfare of his fellow man. No one is unimportant.

In quiet places, reason abounds... in quiet people there is vision and purpose... many things are revealed to the humble that are hidden from the great.

Sleep peacefully, Adlai. There is hope yet. Isn't there?

WINDMILLS

The windmill on Homer Hansen's farm is the tallest flowering weed in McHenry County. It's also a prairie landmark, a proud monument to the American family farm. But now that farmer Hansen is dead and the farm has been sold, the new owner from the big city, his dollar-mad brain already picturing ten rows of tract houses, says, "Cut that ugly thing down as soon as you can get to it, boys. I'll have no use for that on *my* property. Say, what do they call them things, anyway?"

*

The saddest sight I've seen all day is an old and abandoned windmill near Charleston, Illinois, its tail vane smashed, its fan blades broken and hanging down. No longer will anyone be able to listen to the creak and groan of this wonderful country contraption on a windy April morning when the whole state is about ready to turn warm and green again.

*

One could be a lot worse than a passionate lover of windmills.

SOME SMART REMARKS ON THE CLOSING OF THE HIRAM WALKER DISTILLERY IN PEORIA

I was no help at all, being a Jack Daniel's drinker from way back, and before that a Jim Beam or Old Crow drinker, and before that, in the tenth grade, an Early Times drinker, that brand being the hooch my old man brought home to ease his evenings away after a long day in the swivel chair down to the Courthouse. Holy Toledo, I thought those Walker people would be in Peoria forever. Like I say, I drank other brands, but I didn't mind them making their own stuff. I'd be in a bar someplace having a few drinks and maybe shooting some pool, and I'd see the bartender take down the Walker, and I'd say to myself, "Some old dude is going to have himself some Peoria whiskey tonight." No, I was no help at all.

It would seem that what we got in this country nowadays is too many young folks on pot and Pepsi Cola, and too many old folks on blackberry wine and light beer.

Before Doreen went on the wagon, she drank nothing but Peoria whiskey. Believe me, it wasn't easy for her to watch her alcohol alma mater go down the drain, and she being helpless to do anything to help save them, being confined by the AA to milkshakes and Seven-Up. Pity.

ELIZABETH REED

The first woman to be executed in Illinois was Elizabeth Reed, who was tried, convicted, and hanged in public for poisoning her husband so that she might marry another man. The place was Lawrenceville, the county seat of Lawrence County. The time was 1845. I don't know what kind of married life the Reeds had. I don't know if her husband was cruel and abusive to her, or if she was nasty and bitchy to him. I don't know anything about the man she wanted to marry so desperately that she would resort to murder. What I do know is that in Lawrenceville, in 1845, the gallows was probably the only place where men and women were treated as equals. A public hanging is a disgusting, degrading spectacle. Now I know why I have had little interest in tracing my roots. For all I know, the very hangman that put an end to Elizabeth Reed's life is hanging up there somewhere on my family tree.

BARNS

There are, of course, many more barns in Illinois than there are churches. Doreen says they may not be as well built or as cared for, but when you go inside them you know darn well you will have a lot more fun.

*

The barn in back of my place has been around since 1894. It is a red barn with an uncut stone foundation and a gambrel roof. As I look at this magnificent structure, this prairie cathedral, from the bedroom window, it darkens suddenly. An ugly cloud moves over it. The sky is a greenish-black color. Cornstalks begin to thrash about in a wind that swooshed up quickly from some grassy hollow or tree-topped hill on the next farm south. A storm is coming. Maybe a tornado. Now, a rain of hailstones whitens the just-cut grass.

*

I am looking over another old barn, with the fading advertisement: CHEW MAIL POUCH TOBACCO—TREAT YOURSELF TO THE BEST. I say, "Okay, I will," and get out my package and make myself a good chew. This barn is empty now—empty of hay and straw, manure smells, the assorted tools of the farmer's trade. I recall when the cowstalls were full, but that was years ago, in a better, happier time. The old barn waits only for a painter to paint it or a poet to put it into a poem. But for the present, no one loves it but the prairie wind.

*

In Illinois, we have a Save Our Barns Committee. They tell me that they have saved a couple of round barns out west of here. Well, hallelujah and amen, brothers and sisters! Who knows, there might be something left around here in ten years that's worth looking at after all.

IGNORANCE

When President Thomas Jefferson sent his fellow Virginian James Monroe out to the Middle West to look around and tell him what the place looked like and what kind of future it had, Monroe filed this report on northern Illinois:

A great part of the territory is miserably poor, especially that near Lake Michigan, and that upon the Illinois consists of plains which have not had, by appearances, and will not have a single bush on them for ages.

The explanation for this bit of classic ignorance has split the academic community down the middle, one side claiming that Monroe was too drunk on apple jack at the time to know what he was looking at, and the other side saying that there is some pretty sound evidence that Monroe, figuring Jefferson wouldn't check up on him, never traveled all the way to the Illinois country but instead checked into a Howard Johnson's motel in Dayton, Ohio, and spent the time eating fried onion rings and watching the Indiana-Purdue football game on TV.

The moral of the story is: (1) Never send a man who dances the minuet on an important job out west. (2) If the roads are poor, insist he take Amtrak.

LUST

"Say something from the Bible," Doreen said, as we made ourselves comfortable in wicker chairs on the front porch and looked at three good-looking high school girls getting off the school bus down at the corner. "Okay," I said. "How about this: 'Let her be as the loving hind and pleasant roe; let her breasts satisfy thee at all times; and be thou ravished always with her love.' That's *Proverbs* 5, verse 19." "That's from the Bible?" she said. "Yes, it is," I said. "And so is this: 'How beautiful are thy feet with shoes, O prince's daughter! The joints of thy thighs are like jewels, the work of the hands of a cunning workman.' That's *The Song of Solomon* 7, verse 1." "Wow," she said, "the Bible is a lot more interesting than I thought." "You got that correct," I said, watching a pair of shapely sixteen-year-old legs walk up the driveway and disappear into the house across the street.

GRANT OF GALENA

Listen to me, kid. Stay the hell away from Washington, D.C.
—Uncle Mickey

When Ulysses S. Grant rolled out of rolling Galena on an old brass button right into the Civil War, he knew what he was doing. This was his main chance to do something important and he was not about to sit by the stove or go off and hunt rabbits. This nearly ne'er-do-well—soldier turned farmer turned real estate agent turned leather clerk—was born to be a general in Mr. Lincoln's army. He sure made the most of it, all the way to that April morning at Appomattox Court House and his date with Robert E. Lee. But he should have stopped right there while he was way ahead of the game, should have buried any ideas about becoming president, should have hightailed it back to a puffed-up, proud Galena and stayed put. After all, he was a gen-u-ine blue-ribbon hero now and there would never be anyone around the old hometown who would smile and say, "I wonder what tree useless Ulysses is sleeping under today?"

REAL FARMERS

Real farmers have sunburned faces and white foreheads.

Real farmers don't wear T-shirts that say *Kiss Me, I'm Italian.*

Real farmers will greet you with "howdy," "how-do," but never with "how's tricks?"

Real farmers don't milk goats.

Real farmers know all about bank loans and mortgages and the black cloud of foreclosure.

Real farmers don't care if you listen in on their conversations with fellow farmers as long as you wear a seed-company cap and dangle a toothpick from your mouth.

Real farmers don't talk about opera or discuss the plays of Tennessee Williams.

Real farmers don't play polo.

Real farmers say "sunup" and "sundown," not "sunrise" and "sunset."

Real farmers have never heard of Coleman Hawkins and Ornette Coleman.

Real farmers don't drink strawberry margaritas or eat crepe suzettes.

Real farmers know they are real farmers and know that you know they are real farmers.

CAIRO

Oh, Cairo, my old river mistress, someday when summer sings along the honeysuckle vines and slim girls glide down Washington Avenue in their sunshine shorts, I'll see you one more time. You will smile your warm southern smile and say, "Honey, why you stay away so long?" I'll smile too and say, "Cairo, I've been busy up north, busy thinking of you." Then you'll take your pink parasol and daisy-covered cloth handbag and we'll walk out to the observation platform in Fort Defiance State Park to watch the polluted Ohio River bleed into the polluted Mississippi. I'll say, "I sure wish that old towboat there was an old-time steamboat, one of those floating palaces of the old days, maybe even the *Grand Republic*." You will look at me with those sad lavender eyes and say, "You don't wish you had lived back in the nineteenth century, do you, honey?" I will take my eyes off the cheerless river water and look you straight in the face and say, "Oh yes I do, Cairo. Oh yes I do."

GRANDMOTHER

If you had good sense, Doreen, you'd paint her picture.

She sits on a kitchen chair, peeling an apple. The knife glistens in the afternoon sun. She sits on a kitchen chair, peeling an apple. The apple peel grows longer and longer. She sits on a kitchen chair, peeling an apple. The knife glistens in the afternoon sun. She sits on a kitchen chair, peeling an apple. The apple peel grows longer and longer. She sits on a kitchen chair, peeling an apple. The knife glistens in the afternoon sun. She sits on a kitchen chair, peeling an apple. The apple peel grows longer and longer.

Yes, she sits in her kitchen, in her clean white apron, a little flour on her nose, and peels a shiny red apple. She's very old, very small, and very quiet. It's a damn shame you don't know she's there. Or anywhere. But then, you won't miss her until she's gone, until she lays down her knife, after peeling the last ripe apple in the whole wide world.

"Good old Granny," you'll say. "Why didn't someone have the good sense to paint her picture?"

MUSIC

What music isn't is my nephew Jason's harmonica playing. I've just had to endure another one of his Sunday afternoon concerts at his parents' house in Princeton, Illinois, a town where the feature tourist attraction is the home of abolitionist preacher Owen Lovejoy. Among the kid's selections were "Wagon Wheels," "Animal Crackers," and "I'm Just a Vagabond Lover." Throw in an accordian player and you'd be within shouting distance of a Polish picnic, not excluding the usual ants and some brown sand in the deviled eggs. "Do you think I'm getting any better?" Jason said. "No doubt about it," I said. "Lawrence Welk is probably looking for you right this minute."

When I got back home, I put Stan Kenton's *Artistry in Rhythm* album on the turntable and tuned up the sound. It seemed like a good idea, especially since the guy next door had his radio outside with him while he washed and waxed the family jalopy. The country-western station he was listening to was blaring the usual sappy and sheep-dip serenades. My man Kenton blew cornball Conway Twitty away in under twelve seconds. Strictly no contest, and no plans for a rematch, either.

Later on, after a pork chop supper, with lots of sauerkraut, and a brief look at the fireflies sending up their flares of passion and everlasting love, I played about three hours of the great music of Woody Herman, including such longtime favorites as "Apple Honey," "Bijou," "Wildroot," "Caldonia," "Goosey Gander," and "Your Father's Moustache." Also some newer selections such as "Lancaster Gate," "MacArthur Park," "Penny Arcade," and "Reunion at Newport." I was feeling good at last and light-years away from hillbilly ballads and my nephew Jason's mouth organ.

A GREAT BODY

While Doreen doesn't have a great mind, she does have a great body. By the time she was fourteen her breast development was so spectacular that, when she wore a tight sweater to school, the boys in her class couldn't keep their eyes off of her, and many a lathered lad was compelled to retreat to the lavatory during recess or noon hour and play with himself. All through her teen years Doreen kept getting bigger in the bust, thicker in the thighs, and plumper in the ass. There were those who thought she was getting fat, but I thought she was the undefeated sex goddess of Woodrow Wilson High School. I dreamed and wet dreamed of seeing her completely naked, but even though we were going steady by the time we were seniors, all my cunning schemes and clever pleadings designed to get her into the buff fell on very deaf ears. Then one night after I took her home from a wild party—the summer we graduated—she invited me to stick around awhile. No one was home, and she decided to put an end to my agony. "Let's do it," she said, and began to take off her clothes. I did the same and soon stood in front of her with my finest of all hard-ons. After we pressed our bodies together in a muscle-throbbing embrace, I lifted her up and deposited her on the bed. We got down to business and did it good and proper. "How do you feel now?" she said. "Like I won the seventh game of the World Series with a grand-slam home run," I said. "Am I really that good?" she said. "Baby, you're the best of the best," I said. I had to celebrate this momentous occasion and went out to the car and brought back the last of a bottle of white wine. "Oh, Blue Nun," she said. "Very appropriate," I said. "I'm no longer blue and you're certainly no nun." We passed the bottle back and forth until it was empty. "Let's do it again," she said. "Absolutely," I said, and we immediately got going on round number two.

OLOF KRANS

The large framed picture that has been hanging over my writing desk for the last two decades is a print of Olof Krans's *Plowing and Sowing*. For those coming in late, Olof Krans (1838-1916) was the painter of the Bishop Hill communal colony (Swedish) which flourished briefly in Henry County, Illinois, during the middle of the nineteenth century. *Plowing and Sowing* is a simple, uncluttered, unpretentious, primitive painting of plain men working the plain land, plus lots of dark soil, blue sky, sunshine, and some very soft white clouds. In the foreground are three men sowing seed and a woman watching them. The men wear identical drab, gray-green work clothes, brown hats, black shoes, and carry big white seed bags slung over the right shoulder. The woman wears a long blue dress that touches the ground, a matching blue bonnet, a white apron, and clutches a long rod, pole, or staff in her right hand. Above these figures—just below the horizon—is a horizontal line of seven men and seven horses, busy plowing the fertile prairie loam.

I like to think that Krans's *Plowing and Sowing* has helped to shape my poems and has made an impression on my general creative outlook, part of which is: What you leave out is equally important as what you put in.

NOTES ON REGIONALISM

Of course I'm a regionalist. How arrogant it would be to think of myself as either national or international.

*

Richard Hugo was quoted as saying, "I am a regionalist and don't care for writers who are not." That makes two of us.

*

A regional writer is one who knows his or her territory—witness Faulkner, Hardy, Anderson, Frost, Joyce, Cather, Warren, and so many more. The lifeblood of any nation's literature has always come from writers who write primarily about one region, one state, one slice of familiar real estate, and I hope and trust that this will always be true.

*

Andrew Wyeth hit the nail on the head when he said, "I haven't yet plumbed the depths of what's around me. So why shouldn't I stay in one place and dig a little deeper?"

*

You tell me how it goes in New Hampshire or Tennessee and I will tell you how it goes in Illinois.

*

Yes, I'm pleased to be called regional. After all, William Carlos Williams, that superb regionalist, spoke the truth when he said, "The local is the universal." So that's the end of that. Case is closed. Ten-four. Over and out.

ILLINOIS RIVER

There are old men down in Brown and Greene counties who have spent their lives staring at the Illinois River. They are blue-collar men, clear-eyed men, main-channel men, often quiet as sandbars or willow towheads until you get to know them a bit, and they get to know you a bit. These towboat men have experienced all the vicissitudes of Illinois River life, including low water, high water, heat, flood, fog, wind, ice, and snow. All of them can tell you about love and death and friendship and hatred on the Illinois River, and about glorious happenings and terrible accidents. Some of them can tell you rousing tales of the old-time sidewheelers and sternwheelers, when the Illinois River was a steamboat river, and the best show in town was on the river itself. When I listen to the talk of an old Illinois River man, I look into his deep-water eyes—eyes that have seen what I wish I had seen. There are great sunups and sundowns in those eyes, great midday and midnight celebrations. I go away excited, talking to myself, a lost steamboat whistle blowing shrilly in my rivered head.

PIPE SMOKING

It was tobacco that made everything tolerable.
—George Orwell

Yesterday I took inventory and found, not to my surprise, that I owned sixty-four pipes. Some were laying around here and there in various ashtrays and on the marble mantel in the front room, but most of them were nestled in shoe boxes on a downstairs closet shelf. As I write this, I am smoking only three of my sixty-four pipes, all the rest having gone bad over the years—don't draw well, taste terrible, smell awful. I know I should pitch out these burned-out pipes, but each one of them was once a warm friend and constant companion, and I am reluctant to tell them adios, farewell, and auf wiedersehen.

Before I began to smoke a pipe, some thirty-odd years ago, I puffed away on cigarettes. It seems I had trouble holding on to these little suckers. I kept dropping them on plush carpets, car seats, and plastic-covered card tables, and once I dropped a half-smoked Lucky Strike down the blouse of my aunt Lucille while kissing her goodbye at the Greyhound bus station in lovely downtown DeKalb. This is not to say that pipe smoking is perfectly safe, however. I'll never forget the time I absentmindedly shoved a still-lit corncob into my overcoat pocket just before Doreen and I entered an apartment house in Oak Park. "Do you smell smoke in here?" I said. "No, I don't," she said. "There's something burning," I said. "I rather doubt that," she said. "I'm not kidding," I said. "I know smoke when I smell it." "By god, you're right," she said, and we both saw what was on fire—me! I ripped off my overcoat and stamped on it. "I knew you were a hot date, but not this hot," she said. "It's not funny," I said. "Look at my overcoat pocket. It's ruined. It wouldn't hold a soccer ball now." "Don't get burned up," she said. "Ha ha," I said, and knocked the hot ashes from the corncob.

FOG

Fog must not be overlooked in any discussion of our Prairie State weather. I have driven my Chevy Monza (and before that, my Buick Electra, my Ford Maverick, my Studebaker Lark, and so on back to the stick shifts of a hopped-up and hell-on-wheels youth) on roads where the fog was so thick it all but filled the inside of the car. Last March, coming back from a trip to Galesburg, I got caught out on Illinois 47 in about the worst example of fog I have ever seen. I should have pulled off the road, but I kept going, kept creeping along, half out of stupid stubbornness, half out of pathetic pride. I knew I was in trouble when the car hood began to fade from view. Several very slow miles later, my nerves at the breaking point, I rolled into the old hometown. The fog was still thick as country soup when I turned down my street. I tumbled out of the Monza, leaving it three feet from the curb. Fog poured from my ears and nose. "Home at last," I said to the syringa bush and pushed through the front door. "Howard," says this high-pitched female voice, "there's a strange man standing in the hall!" And the woman called me fog-colored names and beat me about the head and shoulders with a fog-colored broom.

BEBOP

After listening to Dizzy Gillespie, Charlie Parker, and Thelonious Monk all afternoon on my stereo, I have come to the conclusion that the most significant revolution in the arts in the twentieth century was the bebop revolution of the 1940s. First called rebop and later shortened from bebop to bop, the new sounds were first showcased at Minton's and on Fifty-second Street in New York City. Dissatisfied that jazz was beginning to sink into a swing and Dixieland rut, Diz, Bird, Monk, Kenny Clarke, Bud Powell, and others decided to experiment with new rhythmic variations, new melodies, and new harmonic changes, all of which were often applied to standard tunes and blues. Improvisation became most important, and fresh ideas popped up everywhere. Thus these musicians added a new idiom to the already exciting language of jazz, and Diz, Bird, and Monk became legends. Monk summed up what was (and is) going on when he said, "How to use notes differently. That's it. Just how to use notes differently." Thanks to the first Savoy and Guild recordings, bebop was heard outside of New York City, and many an open-minded jazz fan woke up one day to find that bebop was the right road to the territory ahead.

At first the national press and the older, more established musicians put down this often misunderstood and controversial jazz. They called it "Chinese music"—and worse. The younger musicians were either enthusiastic at the outset or soon came around. I was wildly in favor of bebop from the start and defended it against all the cranky criticism and reactionary remarks of my friends, some of whom maintained that a hot trumpet solo by Louis Armstrong was the "living end" and was as far as jazz should go. "Nonsense," I informed these timid tin-ear types. "You guys ain't heard nothin' yet." And I went back to the turntable, back to Diz, Bird, and Monk, back to "Hot House," "One-Bass Hit," "Groovin' High," "Off Minor," "Salt Peanuts," "Well You Needn't," and "Oop Bop Sh'Bam."

PARADE

The year I rode a horse in our Fourth of July parade, it was hot, hot, hot. The temperature on the electric sign outside the Farmers and Merchants National Bank showed an even 100 degrees. Old ladies were fanning themselves with anything they could get their hands on, and most of the boys and girls wore as little as the law would allow. The guys on the new fire truck in front of me were mopping their brows with sweat-soaked handkerchiefs. But, you know, it was strange. All the time I was guiding my palomino, *Sunshine's Command*, down muggy Main Street, I was lost in my own world, and this world was cold, cold, cold. I was walking along Main Street. The driving snow was diving under my overcoat collar. My hands were numb inside my thin leather gloves. The boots I wore were lead weights. "Blizzard," says Dexter Gates, the town druggist, locking his store. "No day for parades," I tell him, and continue on my way home, bending forward into the arctic wind like a skier on a steep slope at Sun Valley.

DECATUR

Once upon a time, in wide-eyed 1958, I spent a night in Decatur, Illinois, the self-proclaimed "Soybean Capital of the World." The next day, I shook hands with four midgets on the main drag. They said they were carnival performers, drumming up business for a show. Ever since that time I have always thought of Decatur as the "Midget City," the city of the short, where everything is small and wee and tiny, where the key to the city is the size of a hairpin, and the president of the bank is so puny he can pace up and down under his bed. Of course there are many people living there who are anything but diminutive, let alone midgets, and who think of the place as a pretty hot-stuff town, once the home territory of the young Abraham Lincoln, who, at a strapping 6 feet 4 inches, was a bona fied giant in those days. But small and large matters seldom worry anyone in Decatur, Illinois. Good grief and golly gee whiz, when you are the "Soybean Capital of the World," you can relax, loosen your tie, and put in many a carefree evening playing euchre and seven-card stud over at the Elks Club. You see, there is nothing to fret yourself about once you have scaled the heights, reached the big time.

ALTON'S GIANT

When you are talking about real Prairie State giants, Abe Lincoln is not even in the picture. So let's turn our attention to Alton, Illinois, the hometown of one Robert Wadlow, a fine specimen of American manhood if there ever was one. Bob stood a towering 8 feet 11 inches in his argyle socks, making him the tallest hombre who ever lived. Not only super tall, he was also super heavy, and, at 439 pounds, he no doubt had to weigh himself down at the feed store. The man would have been a real sketch to watch in an upper berth of the *Broadway Limited.* Wadlow died in 1940, at the age of twenty-two, thus missing the golden opportunity of bouncing a basketball off the top of Wilt ("The Stilt") Chamberlain's head. With the big fellow gone from the Alton scene, there must have been a lot more room on the sidewalks, especially downtown during the January white sales. I'll bet he was missed, too. He would have been my friend. I've never known a giant I didn't like.

THE UPPER CRUST

When the kid had his first birthday, they naturally had to throw a big party—lots of presents, ice cream and cake, and some relatives in from Lake Forest and Winnetka. They put the kid in his highchair, tied on a bib featuring a plump red chicken, and got ready to put on funny hats and begin the festivities. It was a hot day in the middle of a hot summer and a squadron of flies was on maneuvers in the house, thanks to the soft-water man who kept the screen door open while he was flirting with the maid. Flyswatters were rounded up and some pretty heavy swatting began. But the flies, knowing there was ice cream and cake on the table, were much too quick, and there were few casualties. "Hey, I know, get Quentin," someone said. Quentin was a mentally-retarded boy who lived down the street. He was a likable young man, but he drooled a lot and most people in the neighborhood didn't feel comfortable when he came around. They thought someone should put him in some kind of institution. Quentin possessed the quickest pair of hands this side of the Continental Divide, and he proved this all over again when he appeared on the birthday scene. *Slap, slap, slap*, and there were dead flies all over the dining room. Everyone smiled and a heavily-jeweled aunt clapped wildly. "Thanks much, Quentin, old boy," they said. "Come back in an hour or so and if there is any cake left, we will be most happy to let you have a piece. Just scratch on the screen door." Quentin drooled on the oriental rug and looked like he was going to cry. He walked out of the house, but held the screen door open so more flies could get in and make for the cake. Seeing this, the maid laughed. "Quick Hands" Quentin had made her day.

ROCKFORD

Rockford? Why write about Rockford? Well, I'll be honest about it. I wouldn't be writing about Rockford if my mother hadn't been born there, on November 20, 1894. Her father pulled up stakes in Springfield, Missouri, one day and hustled his family (one wife, one son, one daughter) to this city on the Rock River. He was a piano tuner, and word must have leaked out that there were lots of pianos that needed tuning up there in the Prairie State. I don't think my mother cared too much about pianos—or any other musical instrument, including the bassoon, the bagpipe, and the bass drum, not to mention the xylophone. "The xylophone?" Doreen says. "I said not to mention the xylophone," I say. My mother never played the piano—tuned or untuned—and we never had one in the house when I was growing up. She died when I was fairly young, so we never got around to talking about pianos, let alone Grandfather's piano-tuning days. And as for Rockford, I never heard a word about it. I guess it's not very important where you're born. Take Doreen, for an example. She was born in Cody, Wyoming. You can stick bamboo shoots under her toenails and she still wouldn't be able to pass out any information on that town.

MIDWINTER THOUGHTS

About John Peter Altgeld (1847-1902), the great reform governor of Illinois in the 1890s, a man who put principle before politics and popularity, who courageously and correctly pardoned three of the Haymarket anarchists because they did not receive a fair trial, who protested the use of federal troops during the Pullman strike in 1894, who was a great and active friend of higher education, who was, in Clarence Darrow's words, "The voice for the weak, the maimed, the defenseless, the voiceless, all over America, a soldier in the everlasting struggle of the human race for liberty and justice." Altgeld remains today Vachel Lindsay's "eagle," a soaring figure who will never be forgotten as long as men and women insist on their rights as free individuals.

*

About Elijah Lovejoy (1802-1837), the Abolitionist newspaper editor of Alton, Illinois, who was murdered when he tried to prevent the destruction of his printing press by a pro-slavery mob. In one of the very worst cases on record of the miscarriage of justice in America, those who shot and killed Lovejoy were acquitted. Nevertheless, his death kindled a hot fire under the antislavery movement.

*

About Black Hawk (1767-1838), the celebrated chief of the Sauk and Fox Indians, who refused to stay put in Iowa where he was exiled when his homeland in northwest Illinois was invaded by white settlers, and who recrossed the Mississippi River with his followers, which included women and children, with the intention of resettling in his home state, white man or no white man. This gutsy action brought on the Black Hawk War, in 1932, which ended badly for the Indians, most of whom were butchered by government troops. Black Hawk was taken prisoner and incarcerated for awhile. The chief was a smart man. He was one of the first to recognize the fact that Illinois is a better place to live than Iowa.

CATALPA

It's the love and kisses tree. It's the tree of young romance and the bittersweet memory of young romance, of hand-holding moonlit walks down a deserted Main Street after the last dreamy waltz at the outdoor dance. It's the hugging tree of please be mine, of let's stay together for all time. Its huge heart-shaped leaves are green valentines, to be given away to the one you love best. Its clusters of white, bell-shaped flowers, their throats streaked with yellow and sprinkled with purple, are a June bride's bouquet, which Doreen caught yesterday in a warm, wedding-band wind.

LADY WRESTLER

Doreen is a professional lady wrestler now. I have a large glossy photograph of her in her wrestling outfit handing up in my den. At twenty-eight, standing 5 feet 8 inches, her once trim waistline is gone forever. She says she weighs 210 pounds, stripped, and I believe her. The photograph reveals massive thighs exploding below wide hips. Her breasts bulge hugely in what is no doubt a 44 D-cup brassiere. Her shoulders and arms are big and very muscular. She wrestles all over the world. Picture postcards arrive from Montreal, Hamburg, Mexico City, Honolulu. The last issue of a wrestling magazine had six pages of action pictures, taken at a recent championship match in Tokyo between Doreen and a Japanese teenage girl who wears a white mask and who, according to the article, weighs 235 pounds. The photos show how Doreen won the one-fall event after twenty-nine minutes of very sweaty exercise featuring side headlocks, wristlocks, spinning leglocks, full nelsons, half nelsons, monkey flips, flying dropkicks, judo chops, stepover toeholds, forearm smashes, various scissors holds, slaps, punches to the belly, some hair pulling, and, finally, three vicious body slams followed by a crashing body pin (all by Doreen), which must have sent out sound waves all over the city. The final picture of the contest shows Doreen standing in the middle of the ring with her hand raised in victory, while her gigantic opponent is lying face up on the mat, listening, I'm sure, to catcalls and insults from the usual rowdy wrestling fans. "I don't quite know what this is all about," I tell her, "but I do remember that you always did like to wrestle."

INTERSTATE 80

Dusk comes on now, slowly, slowly. I pull the car onto the shoulder of Interstate 80 and stop. It doesn't matter if I travel east or west, this road won't take me to my father. I tear up all my folded and refolded maps and toss the pieces into the back seat. I get out of the car and lean against a fender. I relight my pipe. A red-winged blackbird looks at me from a fence post. Farther off, a farmer's yard light shines pale as a child's first tear. An Illinois state cop stops and asks me if I have a problem. "I certainly do," I tell him. "I don't know what day or month it is, or even what year it is." He gives me his "on duty" state-cop stare, the kind he picked up from watching such television shows as "The Blue Knight," "Hawaii Five-O," and reruns of "Dragnet." "This is Thursday, October 5, 1978," he says. I gaze across Interstate 80, heavy with exhaust fumes and trailer trucks busting their fat guts to get to Chicago. "That late?" I say. "I guess I better move on again. I want to see my father before time runs out. He is going to die in three days while eating a bowl of Grape Nuts." The state cop gives me another of his famous official stares. "Do it," he says. "Do it right now." I nod my head, knock the ashes from my pipe. "I will, I will," I say. "Just as soon as I can wind up this frustrating dream."

BARBERSHOP

It's not like it was in the good old days, leave me inform you gents of that right now. Just this very afternoon, I was in the local barbershop, about halfway through the usual—shampoo, haircut, neck shave, a few drops of Lucky Tiger, scalp massage, some talcum powder around the edges, a quick brushing with the whisk broom—when this teenage girl strolls in, somewhere in the middle of a real dirty story, something about a sea captain's wife and a spider monkey. Both barbers and I, plus a shoe-clerk, an acne-faced kid who works over at the Sun Brite Car Wash, and a fertilizer salesman from Vandalia, Illinois, became mute as statues. You could have heard a hunk of hair hit the hairy floor. "Don't stop nothin' on my account," says the girl, wiggling her cute little fanny into a chair. "I already done heard that one anyways."

DOREEN AND GOD

This page had been reserved for Doreen's crayon drawing of God, but it didn't work out that way, Oh, she was able to get God to pose for her, and he told her to take her own sweet time. Doreen, however, was too nervous and ruined the picture. Later, she told me that it was just as well because God was very fidgety that day and really didn't look his best—wrinkled suit, mud-stained boots, a little dried egg on his vest—due to his current worries concerning nuclear war and the rumored rumblings of dangerous discontent going on in some of the other suicidal planets.

TOUGH LUCK IN QUINCY

"There is something here to write about," I say to myself, looking down at this clean-shaven man in a well-pressed blue suit, asleep under a sycamore tree in the public park, the pages of the *Quincy Herald-Whig* scattered about him, orange peels piled neatly near his left shoe, half a cigar stuck in his mouth. This guy is obviously no bum, no wobbly-legged wino. I would like to get his story, but I'm not going to wake him up and start badgering him with questions like some eager-beaver journalist from the Associated Press. He is probably taking a mid-morning nap on a nice day, no more than that. Nevertheless, I wouldn't be at all surprised if he wasn't another victim of the Reagan Depression (brought about by the carefully crafted campaign to help the rich and screw the poor), a good man without even a bad job. Sure, notice the folded and marked-up want ads page of the *Quincy Herald-Whig*. I'll come back later, and if he's awake, I'll say, "I know all about it, buddy. I'm unemployed too. Now let's go somewhere and eat a bowl of soup or, if you'd rather, drink a beer or two." I think he and I would get on pretty well, and I would get my story, some real-life stuff I can use in a poem to tell the world that there is also plenty of tough luck in Quincy.

GRAIN ELEVATOR

It was one of those sunny, shiny penny, slicked-back mornings in the middle of May. The purple and white lilacs were in full bloom and the soft breeze smelled like homemade bread and just-ironed clothes. "What are you doing today?" Doreen said, when I came out of Butterfield's Bakery carrying a sack of still-warm jelly doughnuts. "Well," I said, "I'm going down to see the new grain elevator by the Chicago and North Western tracks and ask somebody how tall it is, and how many bushels of corn it holds, and could I see if there's anything stored there now?" She gave me her best Doreen smile—the one she used to get an A in English from old man Engstrom—and squeezed my arm. I spread my right hand over her blue-jeaned left buttock and rubbed it gently. "Does that mean you want me to come along?" she said. "I wouldn't have it any other way, lover," I said, reaching for a jelly doughnut.

POETRY WORKSHOP

No, I never attended the University of Iowa's famous poetry workshop, and I didn't go to Stanford or Cornell to learn my craft, either. I took my verse training at good old Burma-Shave U, which featured a sprawling campus that stretched from coast to coast and provided unlimited parking. It was a unique experience—no tuition, no homework, no Rose Bowl game. While Pop was steering the family transportation along the dusty highways of Great Depression America (my mom studying a roadmap, my sister changing clothes on a Shirley Temple doll), I went to work memorizing the shaving-cream signs. Yes, I can still recall some of those verse gems:

> BRISTLY BEARD
> OR SILKY FUZZ
> JUST SHAVE 'EM BACK
> TO WHERE
> THEY WAS
> BURMA-SHAVE

> TO GET
> AWAY FROM
> HAIRY APES
> LADIES JUMP
> FROM FIRE ESCAPES
> BURMA-SHAVE

> THE QUEEN
> OF HEARTS
> NOW LOVES THE KNAVE
> THE KING
> RAN OUT OF
> BURMA-SHAVE

GOODBYE

Yet my love for her in its fullness she herself even did not know;
Well, time cures hearts of tenderness, and now I can let her go.
—Thomas Hardy

    The girl and woman who was and is and always will be the lovely and lively Doreen stands in the lighted doorway and waves and waves and waves. I stand on the street corner under a streetlamp and wave back, not wanting to go, not wanting to leave her waving to me in the soft yellow light of the doorway, not wanting either one of us to quit waving, because then we would no longer have each other to wave to.

    Goodbye, Doreen. Goodbye, my true love. Goodbye.

from
LIVE AT THE SILVER DOLLAR (1986)

Musicians play my tunes, but they can't play my style.
—Thelonious Monk

All of the music is out there in the first place, all of it. From the beginning of time, the music was there. All you have to do is try to get a little piece of it. I don't care how great you are, you only get a little piece of it.
—Dizzy Gillespie

I don't mind talkin' if people are listenin'.
—Miles Davis

Keep swinging. Onward, always onward.
—Woody Herman

FAILING

A failing bank in a failing town,
the president of the bank shot dead
for foreclosing on a failing farm,
the farmer, turned fugitive, not caught yet.

The slow hound sleeps away his last days
on the railroad ties of no trains.

A big old boy they call C. W.
says to me in the Harvest Moon Cafe,
"You done using that there ketchup?"

Folks sipping coffee in the back booth
talking on what used to be in town
but isn't any longer in town.

There's the bank president's daughter out there.
She strolls down the broken sidewalk,
cool and prim as a dining-car rose.
She married safe money in another town.

The jukebox snuffs out locals' local chatter.
The jukebox plays Eddy Arnold's
(ah, yes, yes) "Make the World Go Away."

C. W. puts plenty of Heinz ketchup
in his bowl of broccoli soup,
crumbles plenty of crackers on top.

"Don't tell me about no Reaganomics
and nothing about Reagan, neither."

The banker's casket is in the ground now.
Not too many friends came around.
The day is hot and dry, corn withers.
The weather has failed and failed again.

IN HOOSIER DARK

Now what we have here
is backcountry Indiana darkness,
the dark that lurks inside a shotgun case,
plus woodsmoke, rain, and twig snap,
far from motel bar and motel bed.
My messy map to your place
is gobbledegook, piss-poor hen scratching,
a strange homemade sign
in a storm-tossed village crossroads,
half the letters missing.
That is my fault, my mistake.
I can't write right, but I sure can scribble,
and too cocky to know I can't read it.
The local music station
has plowed through two defunct banjo pickers
and most of Nashville's top nightingales.
The windshield wipers metronome the beat.
From the rear-view mirror
the styrofoam dice
jump, swing, and jounce to a square-dance jig
as we bounce along a bad gravel road
in a bad-shocked Pontiac.
Say, is that noise over there
the dull drone of a Farmall tractor,
those figures horses drinking in a stream?
Of course not, of course not,
not at this owl-blinking hour
when farm folks are fast asleep
and rain has slammed shut the door.
Now we stop the car on a wooden bridge
that leads, we know, to nowhere
and listen to creek water
and watch the fog drift through the apple trees
like a ghostly Johnny Appleseed.
Lost, lost, lost, lost, lost, lost, lost.
We are hopelessly lost.

We won't make it tonight to your house,
to your damp, far-fetched farm,
to your cat, dog, stuffed bird,
to your wife with her woodsmoked hair.
The only thing that's halfway funny
is a vision of you at your window,
peering out into the gloom,
glass in one hand, sour mash in the other,
cussing us and the weather
on this Bible-black boondocks night
which, like Jonah's whale, has swallowed us whole.
Man, this is a shame.
But isn't that the way life goes
when the dice come up wrong?

BLACK SUNFLOWERS

In a wreck of cold rain,
a bent and battered
army of sunflowers
blinks into harsher weather,
their time come and gone.
I stop my mud-stained car
by the field of golden dreams,
call out, "Attention!"
But there's no head-snap response,
no strong chins meeting mine.
There are many dark tales
of troops back from combat,
too whipped to give a hoot.
Sunshine soldiers, these.

HOT SUMMER NIGHT IN CENTRAL ILLINOIS

The houses breathe among wet leaves
and the people sweat in their houses.
Along about nine-thirty at night
a train blows for the Main Street crossing.
It has come into town from cornfields
and will soon return to cornfields.
"I want to see the train," the boy says,
coming downstairs, rubbing his eyes.
The train has ninety-seven cars
and will reach Missouri by morning.
The boy stands up close to the screen door
until the caboose click-clacks by.
"It's all gone now," says his father.
"Go back to bed," says his mother.
The people sweat in their houses
and the houses breathe among wet leaves.

THE RAILROAD WAVE

Three pheasant hunters
wearing bright orange jackets
walk along a broken fence.

A long freight train rolls west.
One pheasant hunter
waves at the passing caboose.

The other pheasant hunters,
strangers in these parts,
don't get what's going on.

"Friends of yours?" one says.

STALKING THE WILD WILD RIVER ROSES

We met two years ago this spring
at a frog-jumping contest down in Clarksville.
Smell of wild roses on a river wind.
She shakes her fanny in pure ecstasy.
The black clouds are gone now, gone east
to rain on Hancock County, Illinois.
We're together again, together again.
Her marriage quit in a cold Mexican standoff,
her ex-husband wanting to chase
other prairie chickens, stay out all night,
she wanting wide Mississippi water,
river air, sweet spring in the valley.
"If we can get a boat, we can fish,
maybe off that island over there," I say.
River wind is drunk with wild wild roses.
She goes into a shimmy-shaking dance again.
I grab her around her slim waist.
"Hold this little froggy tight," she says.

TROMBONE

On this mosquito-slapped evening,
the practice notes of a slide trombone.

We named our twins Bonnie and Clyde.
Now, Bonnie has a car, Clyde bought a gun.

Perhaps a new Glenn Miller here,
or just another kid with no trombone skill.

Our Bonnie and Clyde don't rob banks,
but they do worship the almighty dollar.

Yes, a lonesome sound, the trombone.
Also many bleats and blats—ugly sounds.

Bonnie and Clyde plan to leave home.
They both know there's no loot in this town.

COUPLE

A farmer and his wife
come out of the town grocery store.
Each one carries a sack of groceries,
a loaf of rye bread sticking out of his,
a bag of potato chips out of hers.
They cross in the middle of the street
to a mud-caked Chevy truck,
then drive into the country,
back to a cold farm of stubbled cornstalks,
back to a brown creek
where the mist rises all afternoon,
back to a cluttered farmhouse
and a pet canary
who lies dead in a topsy-turvy cage
near the broken hatrack.
Supper is eaten without a word.
The wife washes the dishes.
The farmer reads the paper.
"Damn you and your rye bread," she says.
"Damn you and your potato chips," he says.
Silence fills the house again.
Cold, brown, dead-bird silence.

HOUSE PARTY

We showed up
late at the
house party
and I said
I like him
but not her
and my wife
said I like
her not him
and their door
opened wide
and she said
come in it's
so nice to
see you and
her long hair
was piled high
on her head
and she smelled
like flowers
by the sea
so I kissed
her hard on
the mouth and
my wife said
hello we
can't stay long

BRASS

A brass bed.
I want a big brass bed.
On this foggy April evening
I am digging the brassy sounds of Miles Davis:
"Diane,"
"My Funny Valentine,"
"I Fall in Love Too Easily."
Now there's some solid brass for you.
I snap my fingers, tap my foot.
Of course I'm drinking too much gin.
Of course I'm almost ready to pack it in.
I want to drift off to sleep in my own brass bed
after I hear Miles play
"So What,"
"Spring Is Here,"
"No Blues."
The long evening dissolves in brass.
I want to sink down for the night
surrounded by cool brass,
the bright, golden beauty of brass,
the hard strength of brass,
the soft and loud trumpet solos of brass.
Miles blows "All of You,"
swings into "When Lights Arc Low."
I want a big brass bed.
A brass bed.

THE MAIN EVENT

Saturday morning
and my son and I
are looking at the
wrestling matches on
television when
during a girls' match
the rowdy redhead
lifts up her foe and
with a mighty show
of muscular strength
heaves her over the
top rope and she goes
flying through the air
and lands at our feet
and my son says hey
wow will you look at
the size of those thighs
and I say my god
let's get her out of
here real pronto for
I will never in
a million years be
able to explain
to your mother what
a sweaty female
wrestler is doing
sprawled half-naked on
the living room rug

LITTLE RUBY

We were in the hilly part of the county:
big breasts, bulging thighs, broad buttocks.
My buddy Harry said he was an artist now,
having told them last month to shove it
at Tri-State Liquid Manure Equipment Sales.
We were out in the boondocks because
Harry convinced this girl to pose nude outdoors.
She had a shape like a clothespin.
Mosquitoes were bothering her something awful.
Harry said, "Don't worry your head none"
and sprayed her all over with insect repellent.
I said "Hi" to the girl and she said "Hi yourself."
She had little tits, little hands, little feet.
Later, after she dressed and drove off,
I asked Harry what this girl was like.
"She's not anything special," he said.
"Works part-time at the new K-Mart,
lives with a father who has a wooden leg."
"You ever tried to make out with her?" I said.
"No, no, nothing like that," he said.
"She's just one of your average home-boozers.
Stays home and drinks cheap booze till bedtime."

GREEN DREAM

Yes, I have plenty of matches.

Leaf brown
yellow gray
blue smoke.

Raked and burned, raked and burned
more leaves, leaves, leaves
this unleafed and unlovely April day
than I did all last fall.

April north
is north
of April.

Dream me now a green dream.

BRUISE

He came up to her wooden gate,
ran his hand over the post
where the pale wood had a dark spot,
remembered the little bruise
halfway up her right thigh,
ran his hand over her thigh,
ran his hand over her thigh,
over the bruise, dark bruise,
and said he would see her real soon,
and was there at her house,
running his hand over a post,
over the spot in the wood,
and then walked up the front walk,
and she let him in and said
she was so glad to see him,
and he noticed that the bruise
was gone, was gone, was gone,
and he didn't like her legs now
but kissed her and kissed her
till she said stop it, stop it.

LOOSE

The ax has a loose handle.
The door has a loose hinge.
The fence has a loose board.

Lefty Gomez once told a reporter,
"I had him fooled until he swung."
To swing, you have to be loose.

The Katzenjammer Kids in the funnies:
they were loose kids, they swung.
They loosened handles, hinges, boards.

Loose Lefty Gomez was a funny man,
always good for a laugh or two.
He was loose, I tell you, loose.

PICASSO

When Picasso came
to supper he smacked
his lips and ate up
my wife's baked ham and
her sweet potatoes
and her hickory
nut pie and then we
went out to the yard
and listened to my
seven-year-old son's
tambourine solo
and then Picasso
looked over the junk
in the garage and
removed his Spanish
bullfighter's cape and
said I'm so very
happy today I
will make you people
something real nice and
in seven minutes
we had us an art
treasure made out of
an old bicycle
pump a Mobil oil
can some baling wire
and two green parrot
feathers and he laughed
and said look what I
made and my wife said
thank you thank you we
sure will cherish this
fine piece forever
and my son put down
his tambourine and
said to Picasso
what the hell is that?

APPLE WINE

Poor piece of scratch paper,
it doesn't know what it's being saved for:
a reminder, "Buy apple wine,"
the column of figures that adds to 46,
an Illinois Lottery number,
"Edna, Edith, and Eloise,"
the address of the Mill Race Inn,
a perfect sketch of a perfect tit,
the note that says, "Jerome telephoned from Rome,"
or the three lines I jotted down,
hoping they would touch off a new poem?
I tack the scratch paper
to the family bulletin board.
Let who wants to save it claim it.
I know I won't need those three lines:
Look, the blue train
disappears in blue fog
down the blue track.
Good grief, I'm up to here in blue trains,
and red trains and yellow trains too.
To hell with the lottery and Rome Jerome.
Give me a glass of that apple wine.

LOCAL YOKEL

Wants: to be a big man, wheeler-dealer, hotshot in some wealthy Chicago suburb, expensive suit, a sexy woman on each arm, people staring in the nightclub.

Thinks: I'll go to college, bust my tail for grades, forget pinball, get in good with the right crowd, talk sense, drink scotch, graduate with honors."

Dreams: of returning home one day, snazzy car, gorgeous wife, important job, picture in the weekly paper, snubs for all the peasants who called him "bum."

Knows: he'll never leave from here, was meant to be a local yokel, a county-seat cutup, broke, henpecked, lots of dopey kids with dirty feet.

CHALK LINES

I dreamed I had
too much to drink
and passed out on
the kitchen floor
and then the cops
came in and drew
chalk lines around
my body and
began looking
for clues certain
I was victim
of homicide
and I came to
and said can't a
guy get juiced in
his own house and
be left alone
to sleep it off
and a squint-eyed
detective who
looked very much
like Clint Eastwood
said lie still and
shut your fat yap
this is police
business and you
are a dead man

BURNING PIANO

Nutty, nutty, nutty world.
Flatbed truck squeals into town,
burning piano in back.
Thelonious Monk's "Nutty"
erupts on my stereo.
Local cop Tincup stops truck.
Fire engine speeds to the scene.
Nutty, nutty, nutty world.
There's a brief melody in
Monk's "Nutty" that is so choice
it drives me almost nutty.
I always get up and dance.
Truck driver says piano
must have caught fire from cigar
he threw out the cab window,
several miles down the road.
Nutty, nutty, nutty world.
I watch this show till the fire
is out, the piano wrecked.
Later, I put the needle
on Monk's "Nutty" one more time.
There are moments so perfect
you can't quite believe you're there.
Nutty, nutty, nutty world.

DULUTH

It's
snowing
hard
again
but
inside
the
yellow
frame
house
maple
syrup
is
being
poured
on
stacks
of
buttered
flapjacks
and
the
blue
pitcher
is
filled
with
fresh
milk

TRIBUTE

Columbine blooms in my May-mild yard.
Columbine blooms in my weed-wild yard.

I hadn't heard Paul Desmond's name
for quite a few years, so I grabbed a bunch
of columbine and said out loud:
"Paul Desmond, Paul Desmond, Paul Desmond.
Remember the name, you funky flowers."

The one flower I remember most of all
from my somewhere over the rainbow childhood
is columbine, is columbine, is columbine.
Columbine, did anyone care that you were there?

I bought Dave Brubeck's records to dig
the great alto saxophone of Paul Desmond,
the purest sound in all of jazz.

Columbine, I loved you then, I love you now.

FOURTEEN AND A HALF

When they meet at the laundromat in town,
the woman says, "Please come to see me."

He goes to her apartment the same day.
She leaves the door open for him.

Bathroom is warm and moist with shower steam.
Clean smell of scented soap and damp skin.

She lets the towel fall to the floor.
He stares open-mouthed at her naked flesh.

Dark tulip of wet pubic hair,
the breakfast sweets of large cinnamon breasts.

He stutters, "But—but—but—I—I—I—"
She smiles sadly, puts a hand on his hip.

CHICKEN-FRIED STEAK

"Chicken-fried steak," I said.
"Chicken-fried steak," the waitress said.
"Chicken-fried steak," the cook said.

Iowa: a chicken-fried place.

The kid got fried and was laid to the side.
His chicken found another rooster.
And the party went on and on and on.

Uncle Irving died here in Iowa City.
The joke in Johnson County goes like this:
He died of drink and sex.
When he couldn't get enough of either one,
he upped and shot himself.
"He died without a penny," my aunt said.
"Uncle Irving was a chicken-fried steak," I said.

She kissed me in front of the hardware store.
She smelled like chicken fat, chicken grease.
She was a good egg who liked to get laid.

Iowa: a chicken-fried place.

"Chicken-fried steak," the cook said.
"Chicken-fried steak," the waitress said.
"Chicken-fried steak," I said.

THE STRIPPER

They said wait until
you see the next girl.
You won't believe your eyes.
Oh boy, breasts that looked
like two white socks
filled with ball bearings.
She was an old pro,
legs not so hot,
ass without much sass.
Her "Night Train" was classic.
She had all the moves.
Her finale ended
with both boobs tucked
under her armpits.
Even the hardened
steelworkers coughed into
their shots and beers.
They said I told you,
hey, country boy.
Now isn't that something?

BLUEGRASS BROTHEL

At a brothel in this Bluegrass town,
I bumped into an old railbird buddy
I last saw at Churchill Downs
and a Charley Coke in a plaid vest.
"How the nags running these days?" I said.
"Don't ask," the railbird said, frowning,
two inches of *Daily Racing Form*
sticking out of his chestnut-colored overcoat.
Charley Coke lit up a Chesterfield.
"Give me one word for the new bouncer," he said.
"Try cheesehead," the madam said,
coming into the room with six girls,
all wearing big toothpaste smiles.
"We're off and running," the railbird said.
"That's a good one," Charley Coke said.
"Yeah, he's a corker," the madam said.
The brothel girls were very friendly.
A chunky brunette sat on the railbird's lap.
"The palomino is mine," I said,
and went upstairs with a tall blonde.

CHEROKEE STREET

The man in the brown
coat who is staring
into a pothole on
Cherokee Street
is not a friend of mine,
but the black-haired girl
at the variety
store is a friend
because she has
very carefully
wrapped two old-fashioned
drugstore fountain
soda glasses for
me, and that's what I
have bought in south
St. Louis, happy
as a boy in mud time
with this gift for my
Illinois wife, and
happy too that I
will not soon forget
this delightful girl with
the circus high-wire
thighs and Eastern
European accent,
nor will I forget
the man in the brown
coat who is still staring
into a pothole on
Cherokee Street.

DRAWING OF A HAPPY FACE

The same evening
he was fired from
another job
his child showed him
her drawing of
a happy face
and said that's you
Daddy and the
man said no that's
not me that's not
me at all and
the child bled tears
all over the
crayon picture
she had brought so
proudly from school
and tore it up
into ragged
pieces and cried
some more until
the man said look
here's a little
smile but my heart's
just not in it

THE SANDWICH FAIR

(A guitar piece, dedicated to Wes Montgomery)

We circled the Square,
we circled the Square
seven times looking for you,
but you were not there,
but you were not there.
You told me you wanted to go
to the Sandwich Fair,
to the Sandwich Fair.
We heard you were downtown somewhere,
somewhere on the Square,
somewhere on the Square.
We looked for you both high and low,
but you were not there,
but you were not there.
So we drove off without you
to the Sandwich Fair,
to the Sandwich Fair.

Fair, fair, fair, fair,
we're going to the Sandwich Fair,
to the Sandwich Fair,
the Sandwich Fair.

Fair, fair,
we're going to the Sandwich Fair,
to the Sandwich Fair,
the Sandwich Fair.

Fair,
we're going to the Sandwich Fair,
to the Sandwich Fair,
the Sandwich Fair.

CHARLIE PARKER

Got back from Kansas
City last night and
told my kids I heard
some good jazz and saw
the grave of Charlie
Parker and they gave
me blank stares and my
wife said you always
did like graveyards and
my mother-in-law
said I wonder if
this Parker fellow
is related to
the Parkers I knew
in Janesville and I
stomped off mad to my
study where my cat
gave me a wink and
I said sure sure you
would know all about
anyone named Bird
you sly rascal you

AUNT ALICE IS DEAD

My uncle Ulysses
calls from Texas,
says he heard
from Cousin Candace
that Aunt Alice
died this afternoon
while eating her
daily double dip
ice cream cone.

Old Aunt Alice
full of malice
lived in a palace
down in Dallas
old Aunt Alice
down in Dallas
died in a palace
full of malice
old Aunt Alice.

I say nothing
for twelve seconds,
then cough twice,
clear my throat.
I always hated
horrible Aunt Alice.
"Ulysses," I say,
"did Cousin Candace
say what flavor?"

A BAG OF SEEDS

Nineteen
miles round
trip is
a long
way to
go in
below
zero
weather
for noth-
ing more
than a
bag of
seeds but
our Mex-
ican
double
yellow
head par-
rot has
again
screamed like
a child
in pain
and called
me a
dirty
name and
I'm off
to the
pet store
if the
Wolkswag-
en will
start one
more time

BLUE MARGARITAS

Blue margaritas
are what I drank
in a cellar bar
featuring photos
of Kentucky Derby winners
and gold horseshoes
on the cocktail napkins
then went to the track
and lost money
on every race
including ten bucks
on some Nebraska horse they call
Preacher Clinton
so went back to town
to the cellar bar
with a leaky toilet
and cigarette burns
on the sticky tables
and downed three more
blue margaritas

YOUNG IN TOLEDO

When he was fifty-two
Ted moved to Toledo
and told everyone
he was thirty-nine, and
he dyed his hair straw-blond
and bought a red sports car
and a Stevie Wonder
album so he could learn
all the lyrics, and he
hung out at singles bars
and nightclubs and got to
be recognized as one
of Lucas County's prime
playboys, and then seven
months later he was hit
and killed by a speeding
cement truck while on his
way home from a feed at
Tony Packo's Cafe
over on Front Street, and
his new friends said they were
shocked at his sudden death
and that he was tireless
on the dance floor and was
loads of laughs at parties,
and a barfly said it
was sad Ted would never
see forty now and what
a pity that all the
real fun guys die so young.

DIXIE TRUCK STOP

"Why go into town
to see Suzie Brown
when Suzie Brown
is not in town?"

"The trumpets of Florida retirement sound flat to me."

"You will have to fill this emptiness, she said.
You can fill up this coffee cup first, I said."

"Judge gave him thirty days for contempt of court."

"Is that one? I said.
Is what one? he said.
An eagle, I said.
I don't know, I had my eyes shut, he said."

"Saw W. C. Fields in *The Bank Dick.*"

"Susanna has all the self control
of an old-fashioned rock slide."

"My home atmosphere is bread dough and a harp by the window."

"Stand her alongside Susanna
and your girl won't show up so hot."

"Saw W. C. Fields in *My Little Chickadee.*"

"Ma she don't care
who comes over to eat.
She'd invite two hogs and a giraffe
if they could sit table."

"Hell's bells, he had those county-jail smells."

"If I had known I was going to live to reach 100,
I would have taken better care of myself."

"They got two seasons in California: wet and dry."

"Why go into town
to see Suzie Brown
when Suzie Brown
is not in town?"

RAILROAD MAN

All the time
wears his railroad cap
with the white polka-dots
indoors
as well as outdoors.
Got no wife, no little woman
to tell him:
"Take off the cap, Ralph.
We're going to eat now."
Just an easy-moving guy
from down the block,
a dyed-in-the-brain
railroad man
who likes to sit around with me
and trade
misinformation,
bogus gossip,
I heard it froms,
and just plain lies.
Once had a teenage wife
and a tug-of-war marriage.
A quick divorce took care of that.
No kids,
no family problems
to fret his railroad head about.
Nothing but green lights
down the mainline track.
Railroading again
and again
and again.
Caboose thoughts:
mostly of his squatty frame house
with a picket fence
on Railroad Street,
the grass growing thin
under a weeping willow tree.
But once home,

his thoughts return to
the freight train,
lurching,
clanking,
stopping
under a wide summer sky
puffed with whipped-cream clouds
big as prairie farms.
No regrets,
he tells me.
Says he prefers the railroad
over any woman
he's been cozy with.
Says the current odds
are seven to one
he stays single.
Railroading again
and again
and again.

LIMITED

In the year 1946
the crack passenger train
The Humming Bird
was put into service
by the now defunct
L&N Railroad.
This train ran between
Cincinnati and New Orleans.
I never got to ride on it
because time ran out
for me and for
The Humming Bird.
Also for hundreds
of other name trains
too numerous to mention.
Time also keeps running out
for millions of kids
who have never been on a train,
and certainly not
any limited like
The Humming Bird,
and who keep saying
to their dear mothers
packing suitcases,
"I ain't going to ride
on no bus again.
Let Grandmother come
see us for once."

DAYBREAK IN ANOTHER TOWN

The woman stands by the bedroom window
in her torn pajama bottoms
and looks out at brown crusts of trampled snow.
"Come back to bed, Madge," the man says.
She drops her head, does not reply.
The house is cold, the floor is bare.
The man breaks from the covers
and puts his arms around her waist.
An ambulance screams down the city street.
The baby cries in his nightmare crib.
"Come back to bed, Madge," the man says.
The woman turns, slaps his face.
There's no way he's ready for another day,
another town, another life.

FRECKLES

We are at the
beach and you lie
on your stomach
with your halter
straps down so you
can get yourself
an even tan,
and it's a good
time for me to
count the freckles
on your back, one
two three four five
six seven eight,
that's all, and I
love you, Francine,
for having but
eight freckles, for
you should have seen
me trying to
count them on the
back of my old
girlfriend, oh boy,
I was up to
eighty-eight when
she rolls over
and says that's just
about enough
of that kid stuff,
now knock it off
and let me grab
some of this sun
while it's still out,
and I say well
the hell with you,
I'm going to
find a new girl
without so damn
many freckles.

LIVE AT THE SILVER DOLLAR

Saturday night.
The place is packed to the door
with farmers, merchants, college kids,
and guys getting out of the cold.
The microphone works,
the introduction has been made,
and by golly I am, at last,
live at the Silver Dollar.
Radios all over the state of Minnesota
are turned on, turned up
so as not to miss my first poem,
a poem that will lead
to thirty minutes of poems,
all mine, all going out
live at the Silver Dollar.
Where now is this place?
Ghent, Minnesota, is where.
The Silver Dollar in Ghent, Minnesota,
the first Gopher State bar
to reopen after Prohibition.
I say "Thank you very much"
to the applause
that follows each poem I read.
A Southwest State coed,
"Bambi" spelled out over her left breast,
moistens her upper lip
and closes her big brown eyes.
A carpet salesman
from Cottonwood County,
his hairy hand on a cold jukebox,
takes out an order blank
and jots down the title
of my new book.
Man, oh man, oh man,
what a perfect night,
what a crazy kick it is for me to be
live at the Silver Dollar!

ABOUT THE AUTHOR

Dave Etter was born in California in 1928. He graduated from the University of Iowa (majoring in history) in 1953. After serving two years in the United States Army, he traveled throughout the country and worked at various odd jobs—in places like Cedar Rapids, Iowa; Worcester, Massachusetts; and San Diego, California. He finally settled in northern Illinois in 1958 and began writing poems and working as an editor for several book publishers. Etter has published eighteen volumes of poetry, has contributed poems to numerous magazines (including important European journals where he has been translated into German and Polish), and has had his work included in more than sixty anthologies and textbooks. His poetry has won a prize from the Society of Midland Authors, the Illinois Sesquicentennial poetry award, and the Theodore Roethke prize from *Poetry Northwest*. In 1967, he was a Bread Loaf Writers' Conference Fellow. *West of Chicago* (1981) was the winner of the 1981-82 Carl Sandburg Award for poetry. At the present time, Etter is a free-lance writer and teacher. He lives with his wife (Peggy) and his two children (Emily and George) in Elburn, Illinois.